9-11 is
RED, WHITE
and BLUE

9-11 is
RED, WHITE
and BLUE

Linda Glod

Library of Congress Control Number: 2023906072
ISBN: Hardcover   978-1-6698-7271-9
                 Softcover   978-1-6698-7270-2
                 eBook   978-1-6698-7269-6

Print information available on the last page.

Rev. date: 03/30/2023

To order additional copies of this book, contact:
Xlibris
844-714-8691
www.Xlibris.com
Orders@Xlibris.com
845548

CONTENTS

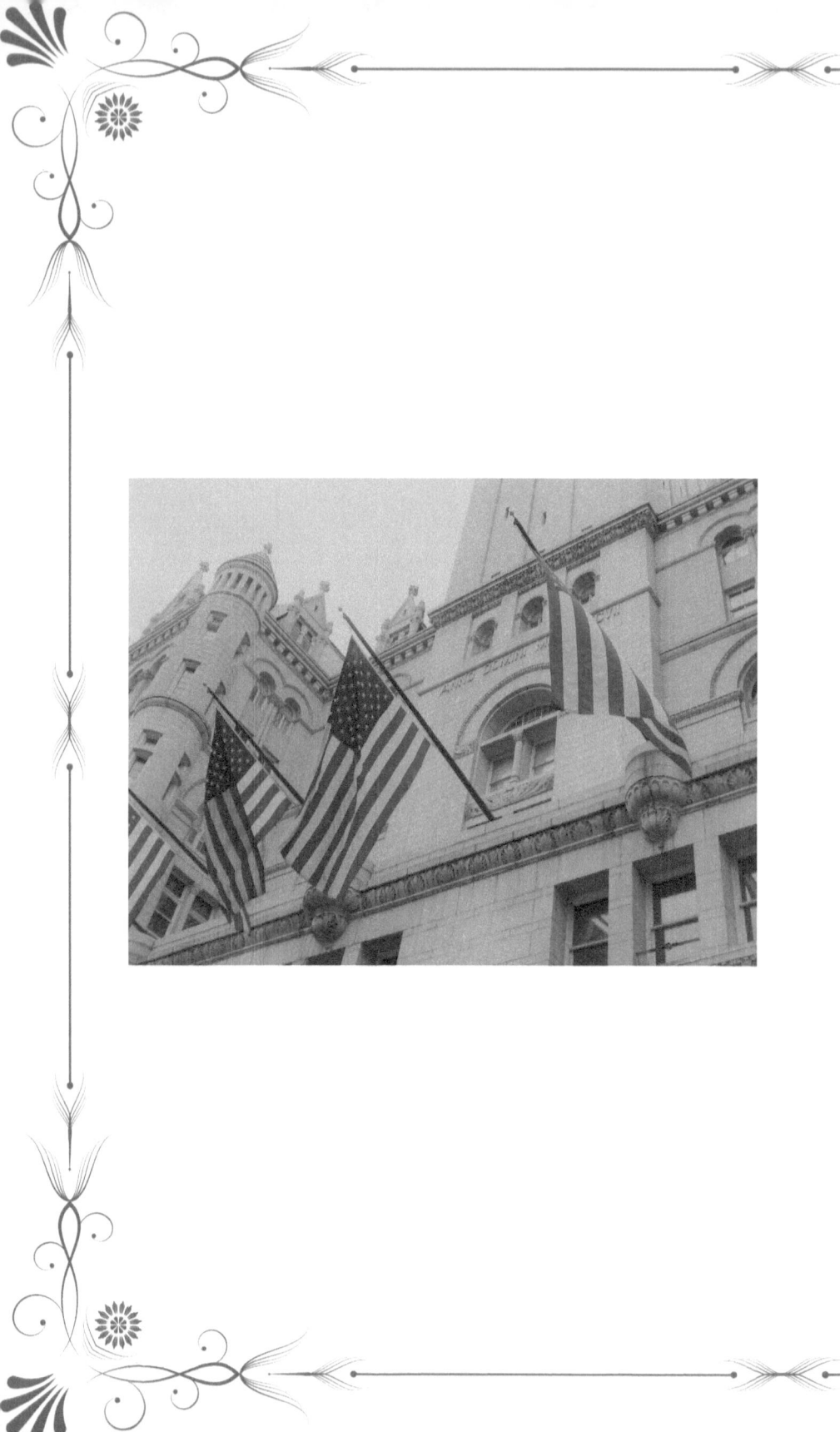

9-11 is Red, White and Blue

9-11 is
RED
WHITE
AND BLUE!

Red rage reacting
Red blood spilling
Red engines wailing
Red lights warning
Red fears pounding
Red fires burning
Red wounds hurting
Inflamed hands digging
Red jaws resolving.

White eyes staring
White ambulance blaring
White soot covering
White coats aiding
White heat melting
White House protecting
White papers posting,
Souls ascending.

Blue skies charming
Blue gray billowing
Blue uniforms searching
Blue hearts mourning
Blue bruises forming
Blue suits falling
Blue lights blinking
Blue phones calling.

Red, white, and blue waving
Red white and blue waving

From bridges
From towers
From cars
From hands
From homes
From trees
From schools,
And churches.

The buildings are not the people
The buildings are not the spirit,
The buildings are not the power.

We are one spirit
USA
Cooperating
Bonded together
Across our vast land
USA
Exceptional
Determination
Competition
Sacrifice
USA
Patriotism
Love of country
USA
We are America
We are Freedom
We are Liberty
We are USA
Loyalty and Leadership
Love of country
Strength of nation
USA.

Yes, America suffers
Whether loss of life

Or alive with loss
Our America suffers.
Parents and grandparents
Children
Husbands and wives
Brother and sisters
Aunts and uncles
Cousins
Partners
Friends and Lovers,
Neighbors,
And work associates.
Yes, America suffers.

Our genes are survival
Our bones are The Phoenix
Freedom Fighters
Liberty Writers
Survivors of the
American Revolution
The Civil War
Survivors of WWI
And WWII
Survivors of the
Korean War
The Vietnam War
And Desert Storm
Battling Iraq
Afghanistan
And Libya
Fighting for Freedom
The red, the white, and the blue
Finding life after carnage
Beauty after destruction,
And hope after despair.
9-11 is RED, WHITE, and BLUE.

A Poem of Gratitude

This is a poem of gratitude
For what I want to say
To praise Prince William County's team
Who saved me one fine day.
It was early Friday morning
Awakened about six
When dizziness and fainting
Gave my plan a nix.
Unconscious on the bathroom floor
And sweating head to toe
Not responding to my husband's voice
There was just one place to go.
He called emergency rescue squad
They were there in just a flash
So kind, so calm, so helpful
To the hospital made a dash.
Destination was Sentara
Northern Virginia Medical Center
Emergency room received me
Immediate care to render.
Efficient, kind, and comforting
They put me in their care
This system of great team work
The outcome I will share.
I stayed a night for testing
All members did their best
No matter what their jobs were
They showed a special zest.
Thank you all who helped me
I'm home and feeling great
As a poet, here's a shout out
"You, I appreciate!"

About Green

Do I like green,
Because it's money?

Or money, because it's green?

I have green clothes
Green candy and pens.

I drink lime Kool-Aid
And savor a salad bar –

My preference for mints is green,
And my favorite word is GO

Which is really a green word
When spoken in traffic lights.

Well – my tennis racket is green,
It seemed to fit the bill,

Because I was a green player
Back then, even yet, I admit!

I live in the Celtic state,
And Irish is in my genes.

So, green comes naturally to me.
Which is why I do like money.

Aging

I'm getting increasingly wrinkled
My eyes and my lips they look crinkled
Trying magic creams here
Having nothing to fear
It must be my mirror that's kzinkled!

Alone on a Holiday

Have you ever spent a holiday
sitting all alone?

Did you look outside your window
both up and down the street?

Most driveways filled
with loved ones cars
folks gathering to eat,
and sit around, and talk for hours
while watching children play.

Now I see back to special times
reflecting holidays.

No need to feel downhearted!

Let memories make you warm
remembering past holidays,
and your driveway filled with cars.

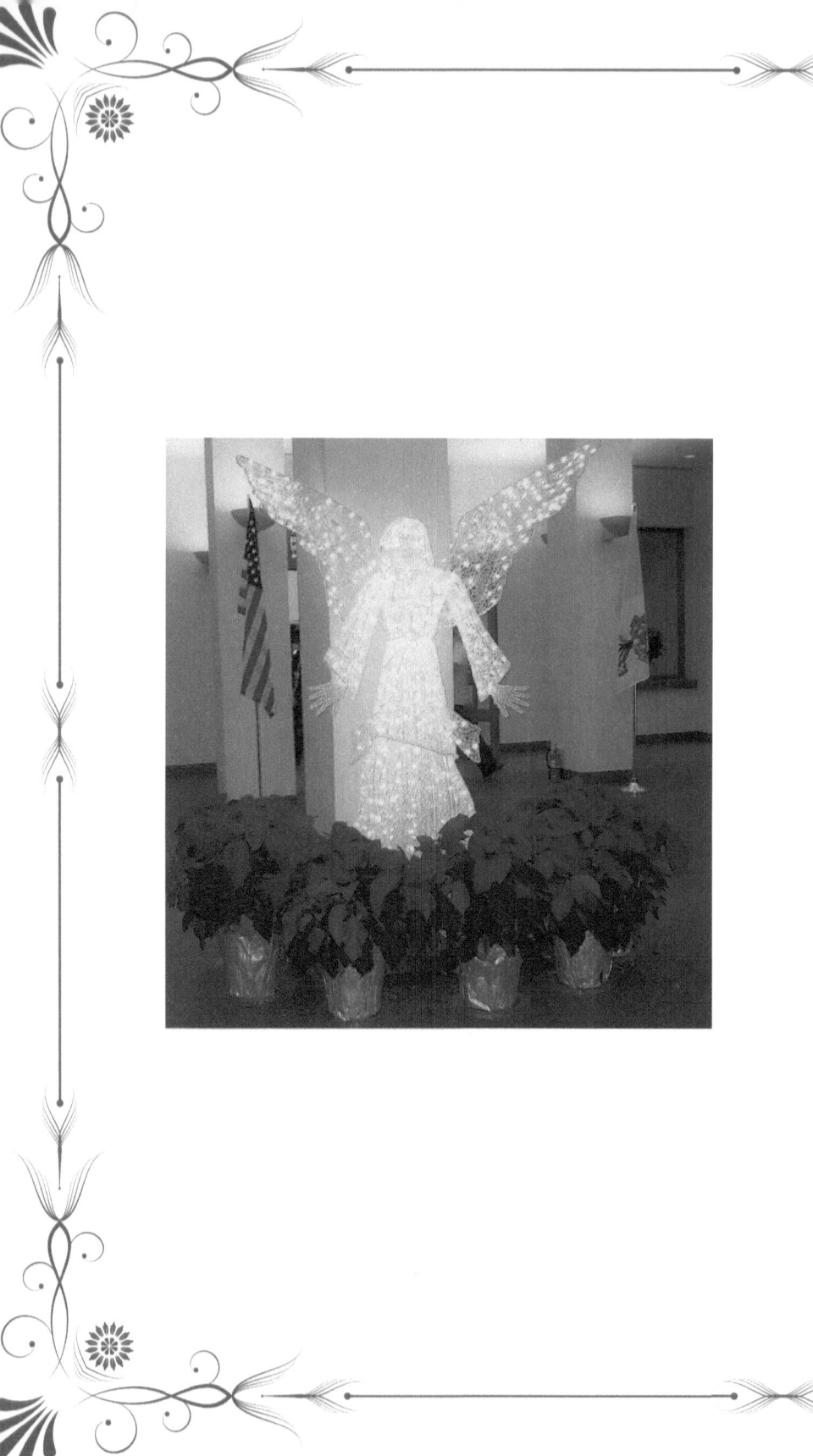

Angel Choir Calling

My mother went to Heaven for Christmas
To sing in the angel's choir
We were planning our Christmas dinner,
Looking forward to laughter and talk,
But this time
We'd not have Mother,
The one who loved us so.
'Cause she went to Heaven for Christmas
To sing in the angel's choir.

At the Pharmacy

Waiting room so fully packed
All ages wait their turn
Small babies and the white haired folks
Each with their own concern
Some coughing, sneezing, blowing nose
I think some have the flu!
I just came for my thyroid pills
So what am I to do?
I'll wait outside to breathe fresh air
And make a call or two.
Check back now and see the screens
I'm getting close, it seems.
My script should come up soon, I think.
And now my smile gleams.

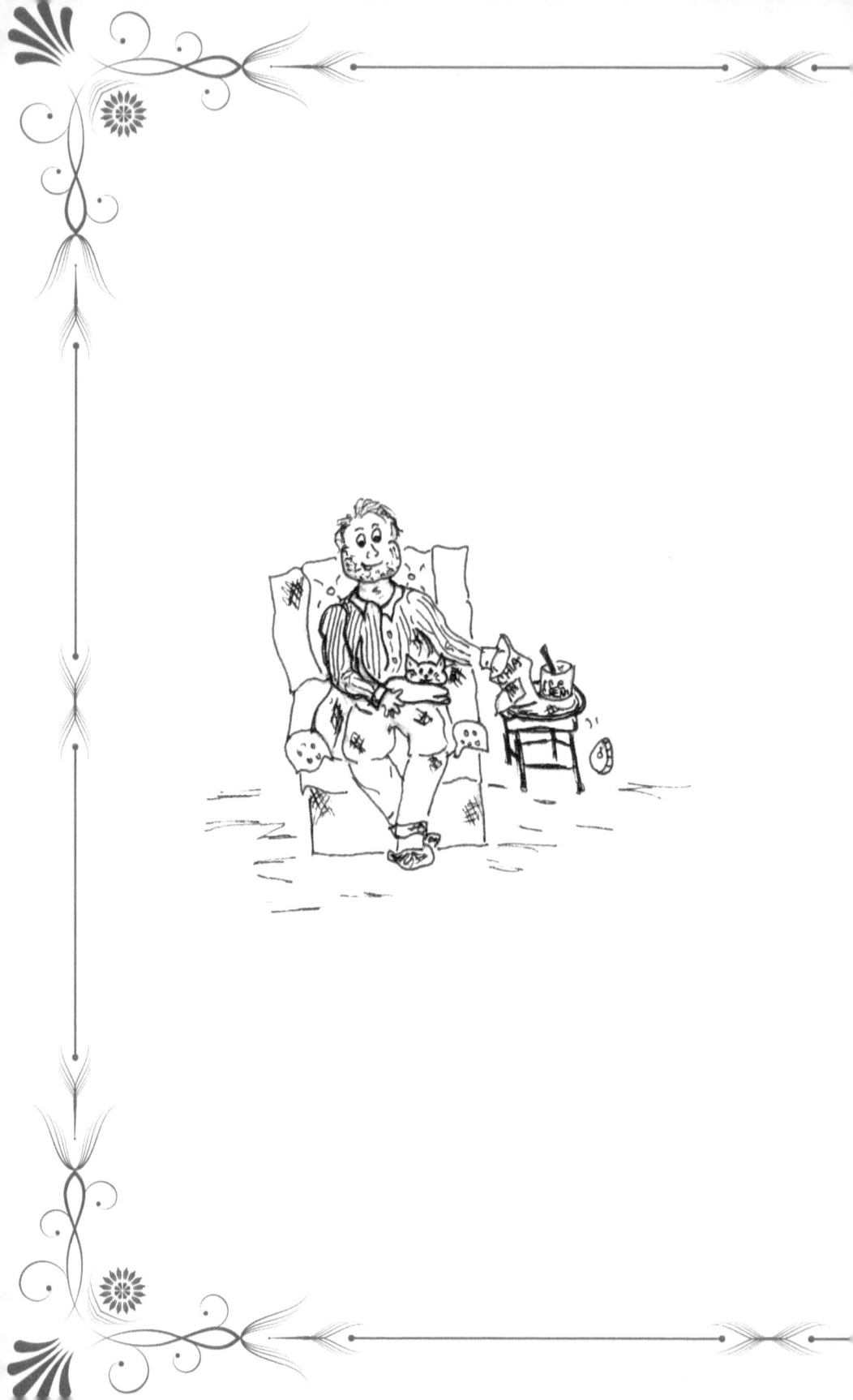

Bachelor and Buzzard

Bachelor and Buzzard
In a D.C. brownstone
Sit by the television
For hours alone
Eating night snacks
Of peanuts or chips
Ice cream and Oreos,
Candies in packs.
They talk in their
Cat-human manner,
These pals.
Then
Buzzard bats Rog
With her playfully paw,
Rog strikes back,
And the battle is on
'Til Buzzard meows,
Then it's jump off she goes
To find a "real snack"
In her kitchen alcove.

Bald Eagle

He flies with perfect outstretched wings
Majestic, he's the bird for kings
Tail feathers, white, he proudly brings.

His head is covered all in white
Large eyes for giving perfect sight
This bird's so powerful in his flight.

Curved talons dress the yellow feet
Large, strong beak with hook so neat
It's right for tearing at the meat.

Today I saw him eye to eye
Such graceful soaring in the sky
Our freedom and power will not die.

Our USA will strongly stand
Let's pledge this oath with heart and hand
WE must protect our great homeland.

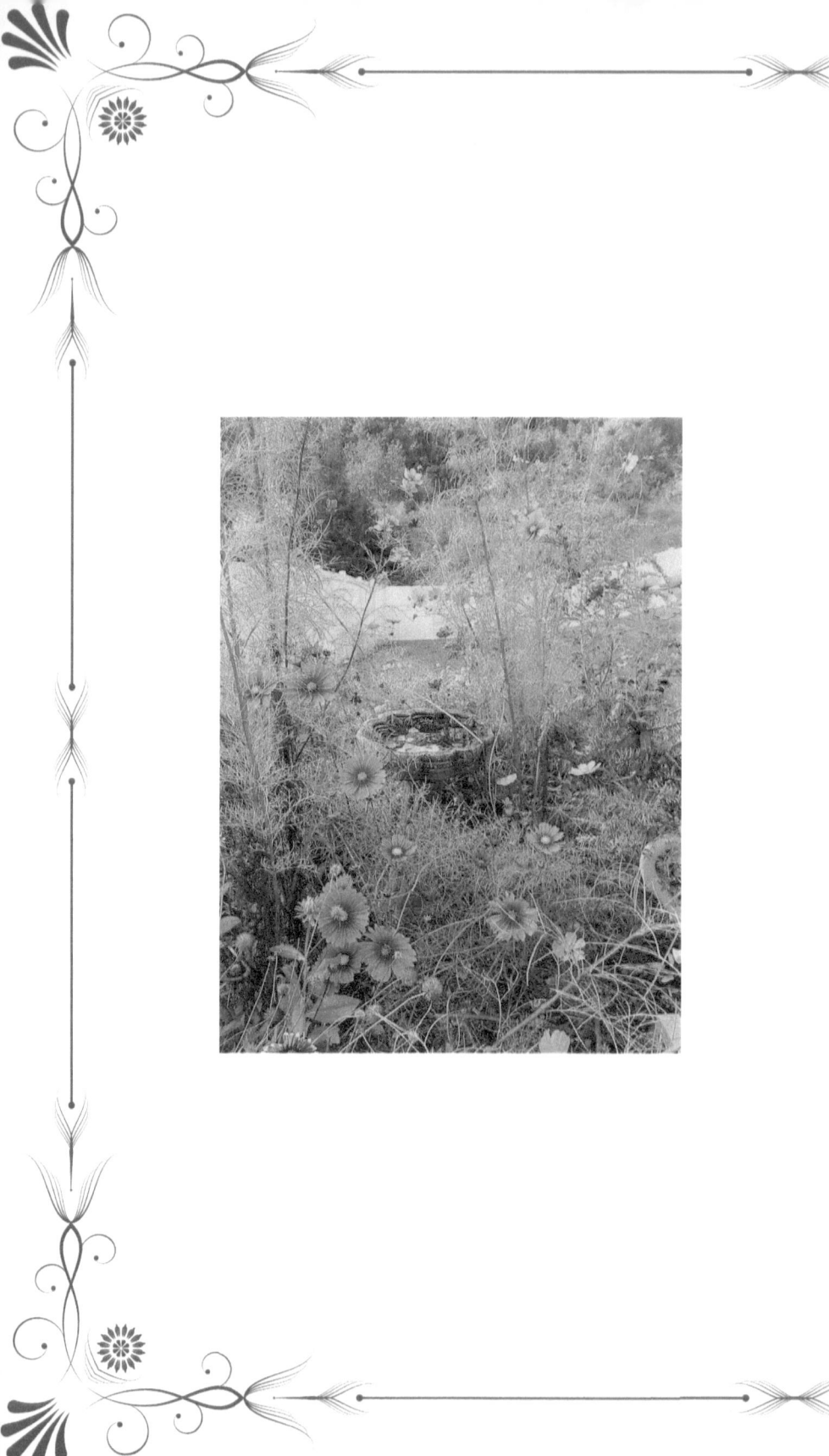

Bird Bath

After the rain
Next morning
Satisfied enjoyment
It feels so good!
Wings flap splashing
Rhythmically
Fresh spring rain
Bathwater
Bird bath
Ready for big day
House hunting
Location
Location
Location.

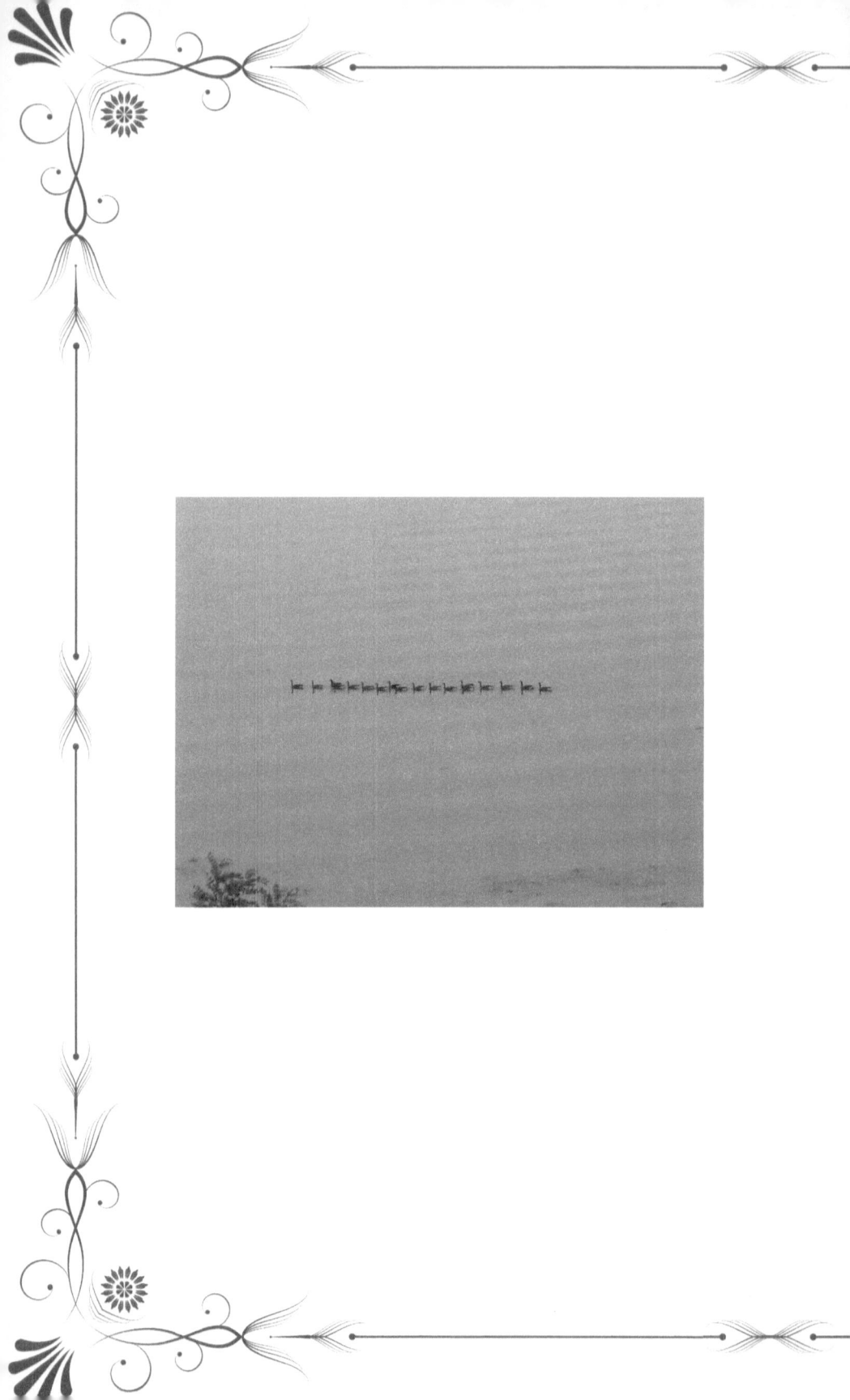

Bird Watching

Mountain bluebird
Perched high on the white fence
Large wing spanned Northern hawk-owl
Zooms in joining bluebird on the white fence
Bluebird watches.

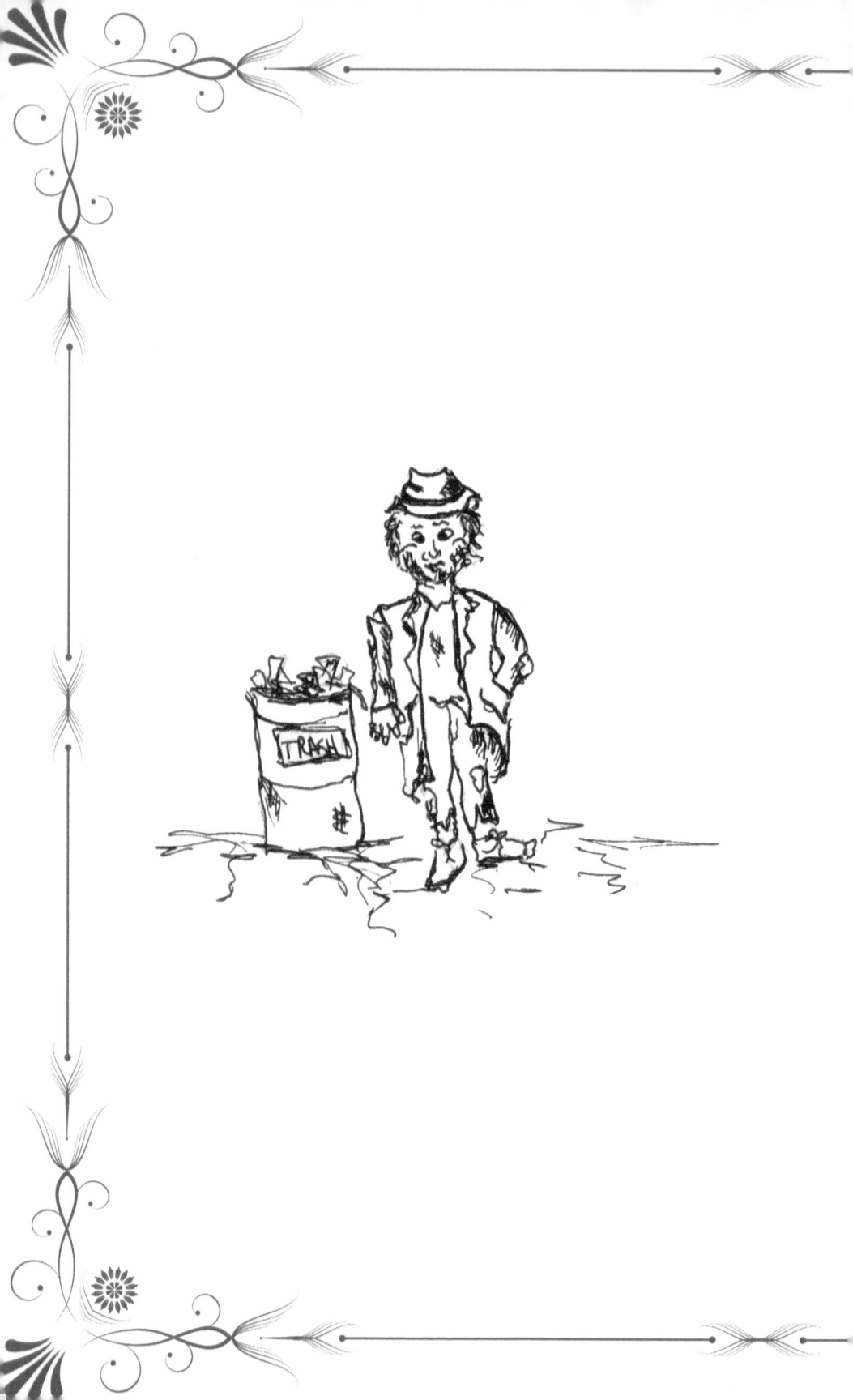

Boston Road Bum

Who are you, Mr. Tatters?
Shuffling up and down the road
With ragged pants and holy shoes
Wool coat in heat of day.
Your mumbling voice
And matted hair
Depict your state e'n more.
Who are you, Mr. Tatters?
Have you no place to go?
What's your story. Mr. Tatters?
What happened in your past?
Were loved ones killed?
Bankruptcy filed?
Did fire burn you out?
Your saddened face
Your downcast eyes
Show sorrow, grief, and pain.
Who are you, Mr. Tatters?
I'd like to know your name.

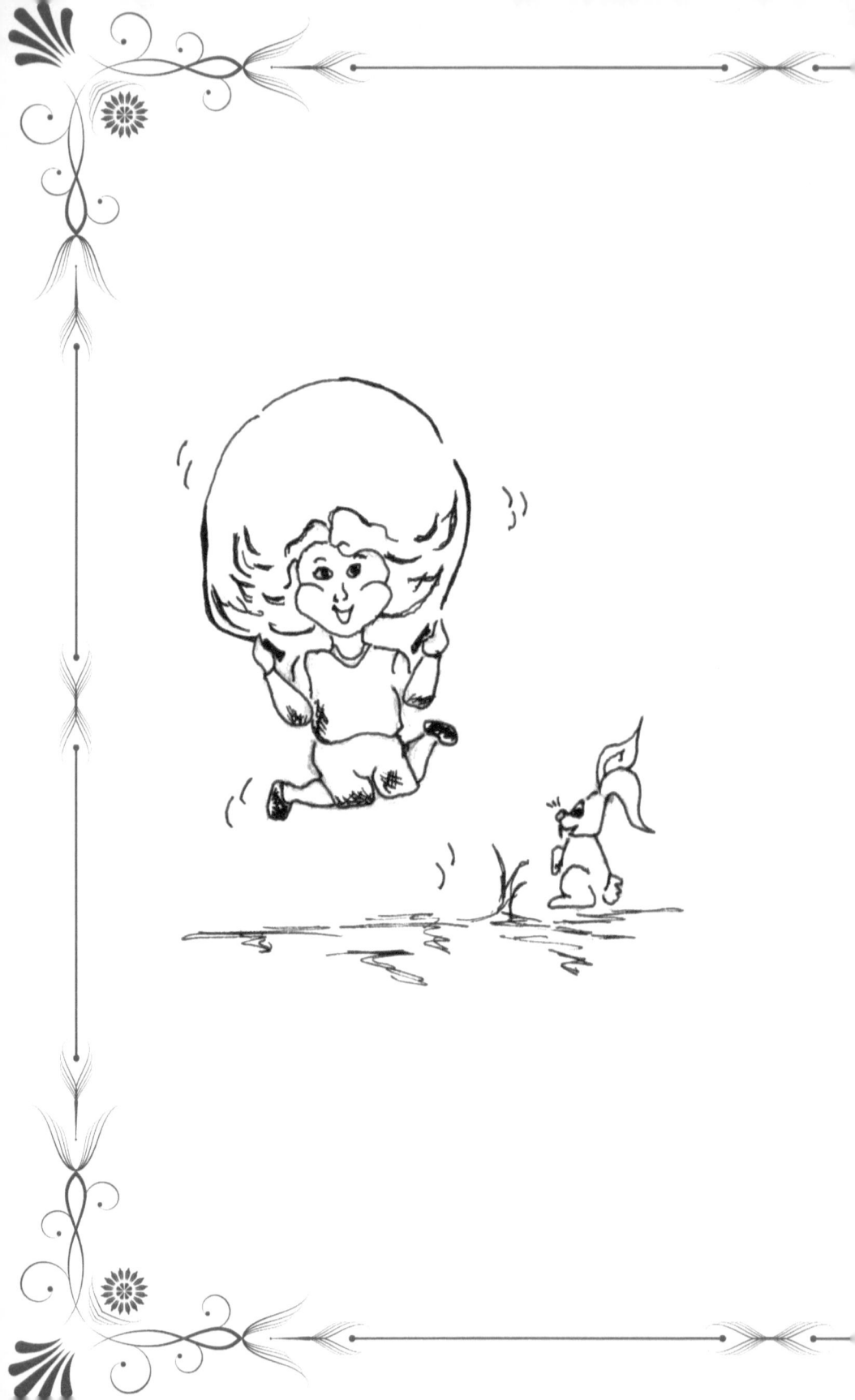

Bridget

Bridget was born with bounce in her bones,
    Rubbery,
    Pubbery,
Bounce in her bones.
She never walked,
She always hopped,
    With rubbery, pubbery bounce in her bones.

Bridget was born with laughs in her voice,
    Giggley,
    Wriggley
Laughs in her voice.
She'd make your day,
Smiling frowns away,
    With giggley, wriggley laughs in her voice.

Bridget was born with gold in her hair,
    Sunshiny,
    Night brightening,
Gold in her hair.
Her eyes of blue,
Always twinkle at you,
    With sunshiny, night brightening gold in her hair.

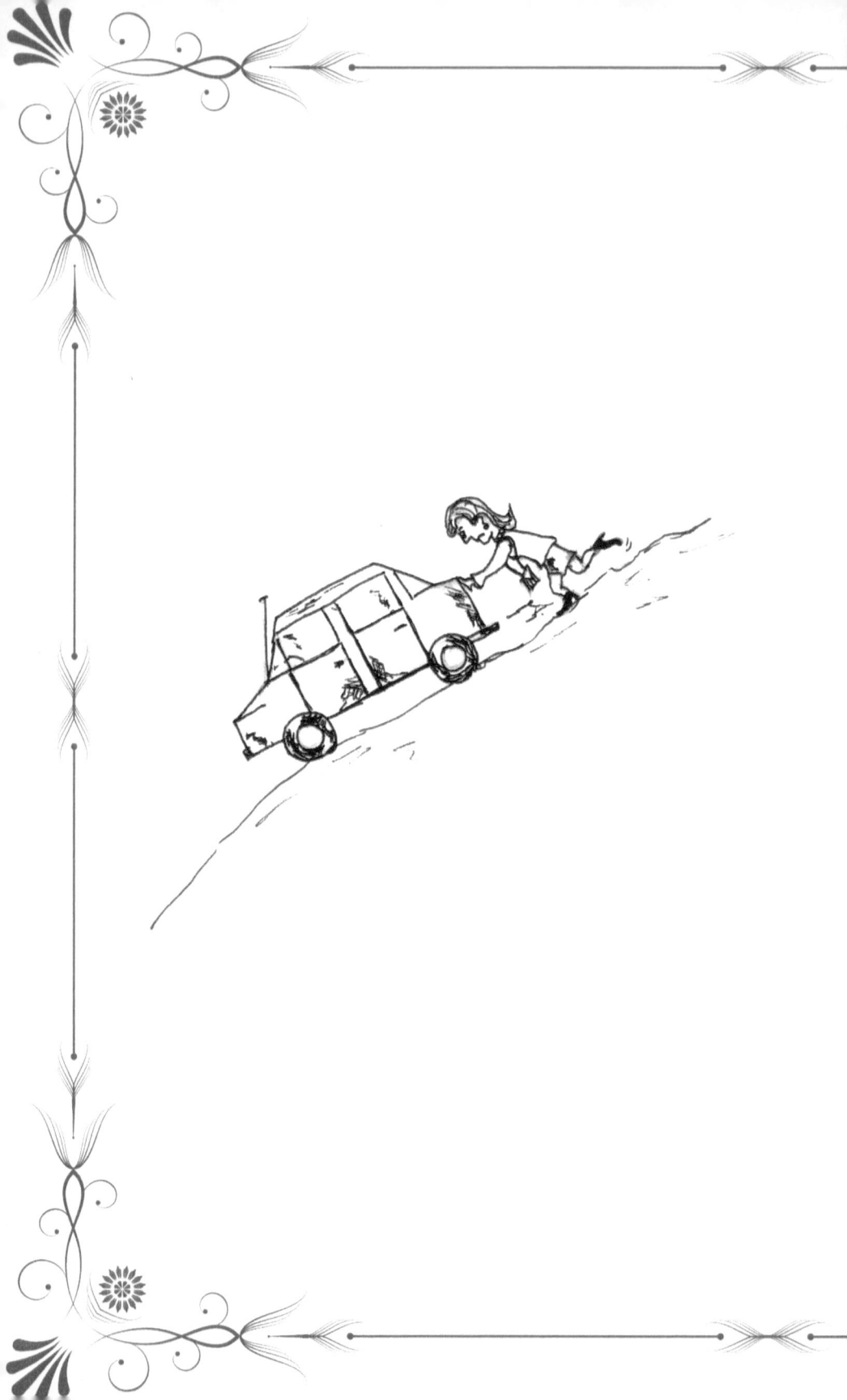

Car Troubles

It's time to go,
My car says "No!"
I try the key
Oh, Lordy, be.

My car seems dead
The battery said.
I'm on a hill.
So, here's the thrill,
I roll the car,
But not too far,
Then pop the clutch,
This is too much!

It gives a jolt,
Starts with a bolt,
The engine purred,
I know I heard
It sigh relief,
Saves me from grief!

Now I feel proud,
And say out loud,
('Cause in my suit
With heels to boot)
"I saved the day,
And got my pay,
Learned something new,
From that I grew!"

Corporate Mind Control

I want to yell
I need to scream
Then jump up high to blast
A blaring blurb of
Barb-ed words

And call them
    Big
        Fat
            Jerks!

But...
I sit in my corporate seat
Serenely prim and proper,
'Cuz if I said
What's on my mind
I'd soon become a pauper!

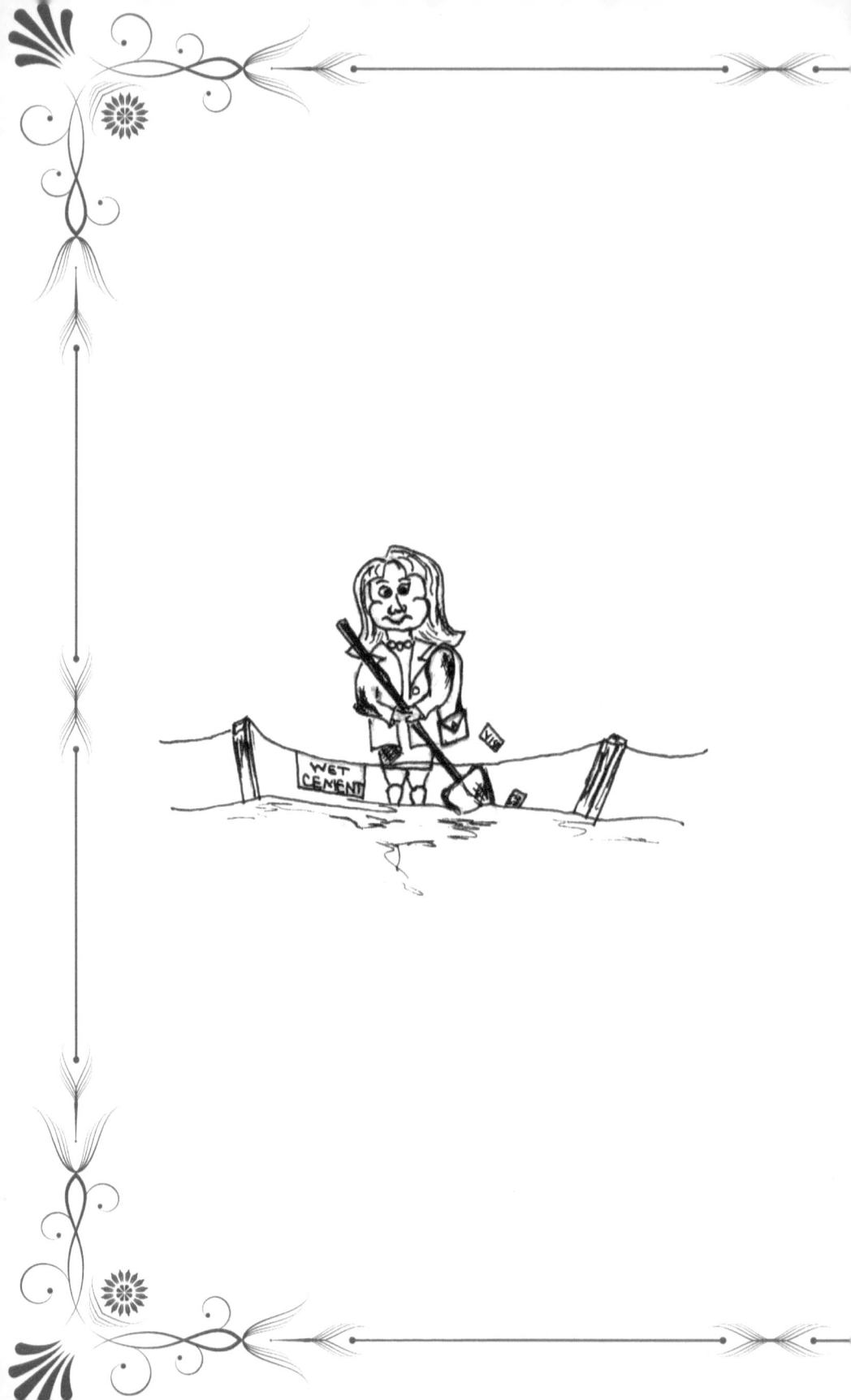

Credit Card Blues

I wanted it all
It looked so fine
I bought it easily,
Signed on the line.
But, now I'm singing
The credit card blues,
No fun on pay day
It blows my fuse,
And it's got me singing
The credit card blues.

Oh, I've signed away
At eighteen per cent,
It's got me standin'
In wet cement.
Hand me a shovel
And I'll dig myself out,
Won't do me no good
To sit and pout!
I signed myself in
Using credit for cash,
Charged the maximum
In a lightnin' flash.

I've got a full closet
Of clothes with styles,
I've got shelves of books,
Large floors with tiles.
I've eaten French food,
Flown miles and miles.
But, look at me now
What a price to pay
I'm singing the
Credit Card Blues today.

I've bought purses and shoes
Antiques and jewels,
Gadgets and gifts,
Modern, specialized tools.
Tried to sew and save
Charged fabric by the yard,
Even bought insurance
On my credit card!

Paid the plastic all off
They increased my credit line,
So I said to myself,
"This is too divine."
Then I lost my will power
When I was out of cash
Knowing that all this credit
Buys a wealthy stash.

I had a barrel of laughs
I lived a "fast lane" life.
But, now I'm faced with
The pay it back strife,

Oh, look at me now
What a price to pay,
I'm singing the
Credit Card Blues
Today.

Deer in the Pond

So very hot it is today
The flowers drooping as they sway

Gentle winds, hot breaths of air
Brought to the pond a loving pair.

A buck and doe with fawn so young
His little life had just begun.

The buck has quite a rack of horns,
The doe is fair, brown eyes adorn.

Their tiny fawn, a curious one
He loves to romp and have some fun.

Both buck and doe now jump the fence
Foliage there is very dense.

Baby fawn climbs through a hole
His parents watch him, they control.

Down to the pond so calm and clear
They wade around and cool off here.

Munching greens along the bank
Fawn stays along his mom's right flank.

Once refreshed, dad leads the way
"It's time to go," he seems to say.

Then off they go the same way out
Their baby leaves without a pout.

I feel so blessed to see this sight
Nature's beauty, pure delight!

DMV

Patience
Patience
Patience
Be ready for
Lots of time
Gobs of time
Oodles of time
Tons of time
Lots of time
Wait in line
Blood pressure rises
Sit and wait for
Your number on screen
Exasperation apparent
In grim faces of
Patiently waiting
Customers
Room full of chairs
So many chairs
So many people
Fourteen stations of
Computers humming
Folks with briefcases
Folks with file folders
Fists full of special papers
Awaiting processing
Employees friendly
Employees efficient
Dealing with
Too many customers!

Eric

Eric, when a baby boy,
Liked plastic keys, a favorite toy.

So, his first word he would say
Not "mama", "dada", then one fine day

My eight month little baby son
Said, "keys", what shocking fun.

At two, he loved to play a game
Adding numbers, he would name,

As I'd hold up fingers high
He would count them! Cutie Pie!

With the cutest baby giggle
And he'd do his little wiggle.

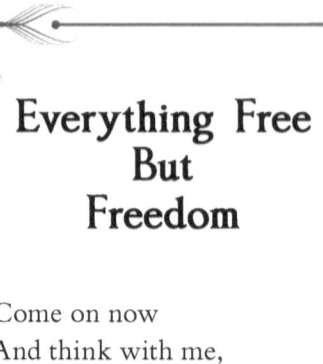

Everything Free
But
Freedom

Come on now
And think with me,
What in the world
Do you want to be?

Would you love to
Teach or preach?
Would you love to
Surf the beach?

What about
Invent the cure?
Go for STEM,
Help lives endure.

Remember
As you make plans
There's a force
To put in bans

    They want everything free
    But
    FREEDOM.

You are in
The USA
Protect freedom
Everyday!

People risk
Their lives to come.
Welcome them,
We all are one.

But wait, now
There's a door
To pass through,
Both rich and poor.

Remember
As you make plans
There's a force
To put in bans

They want everything free
But
FREEDOM.

We're a team
Who works and strives
Go for best
In all our lives.

Feel the joy
Of living here.
We're family,
Now give a cheer.

Own your home
If you'd like to
Plan out your life
That's what we do.

Remember
As you make plans
There's a force
To put in bans

They want everything free
But
FREEDOM

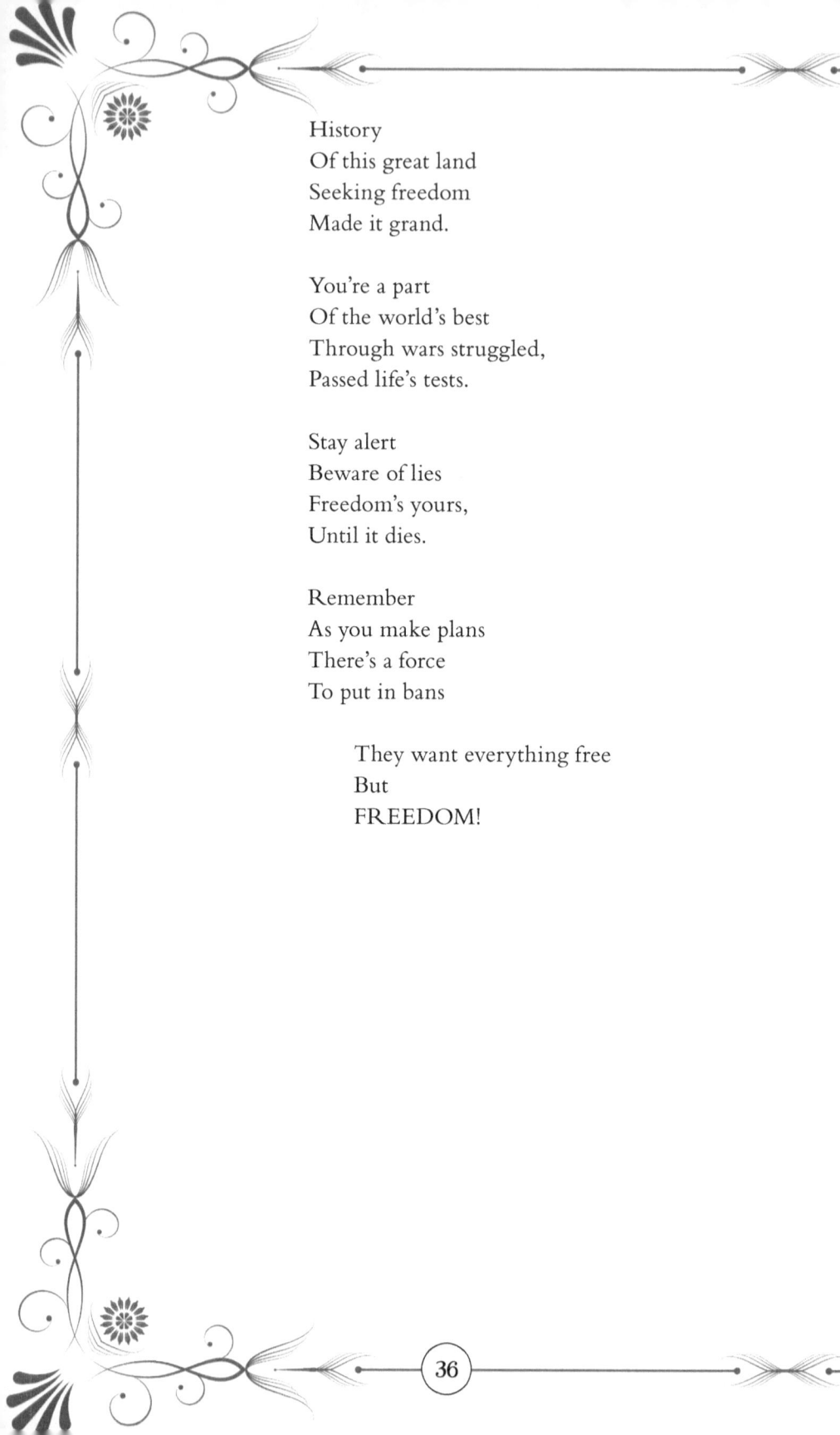

History
Of this great land
Seeking freedom
Made it grand.

You're a part
Of the world's best
Through wars struggled,
Passed life's tests.

Stay alert
Beware of lies
Freedom's yours,
Until it dies.

Remember
As you make plans
There's a force
To put in bans

They want everything free
But
FREEDOM!

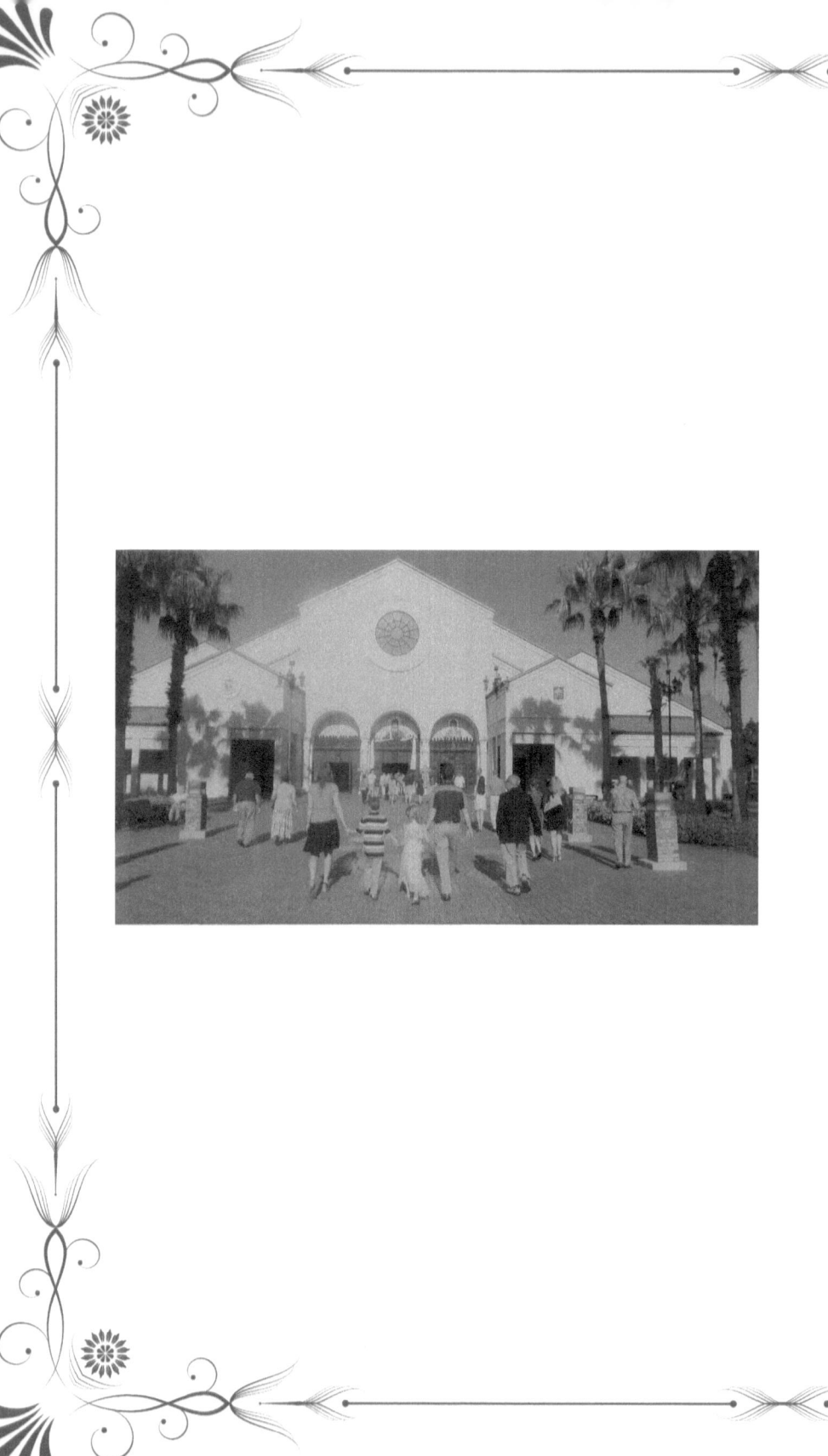

Fashion Springs Forth

All right, now
Here's the look
I saw it in a fashion book.
Feeling hippie?
Grab some fringe
Bohemian's great
So do not wait!

Go on line
And buy some shorts
80's style
Back for awhile.

Be sporty!
Don a surfer look.

Whites look sharp
So crisp and clean
Wear white shirts
With skinny jeans.

Hot, hot pink
To make you blink,
Artsy design
You're looking fine!

Denim jumpsuits,
And tie dyes
Pale pink
Calming, I think.
Love those
Green tints
And animal prints.

There are
Light blues
And violet blues,
Navy blues
And ocean hues,
Metallic silver
To make you quiver.

Yellow is on
Add vintage floral
Bold and beautiful
Add some coral
Found it traveling
Add some shells.
Layering jewelry
Bright color sells!

Halter top necks
And chunky heels
Chain your sunglasses
Then hear the squeals!
Wear crochet,
Midi skirts with style
Dresses with ruffles
You will beguile.

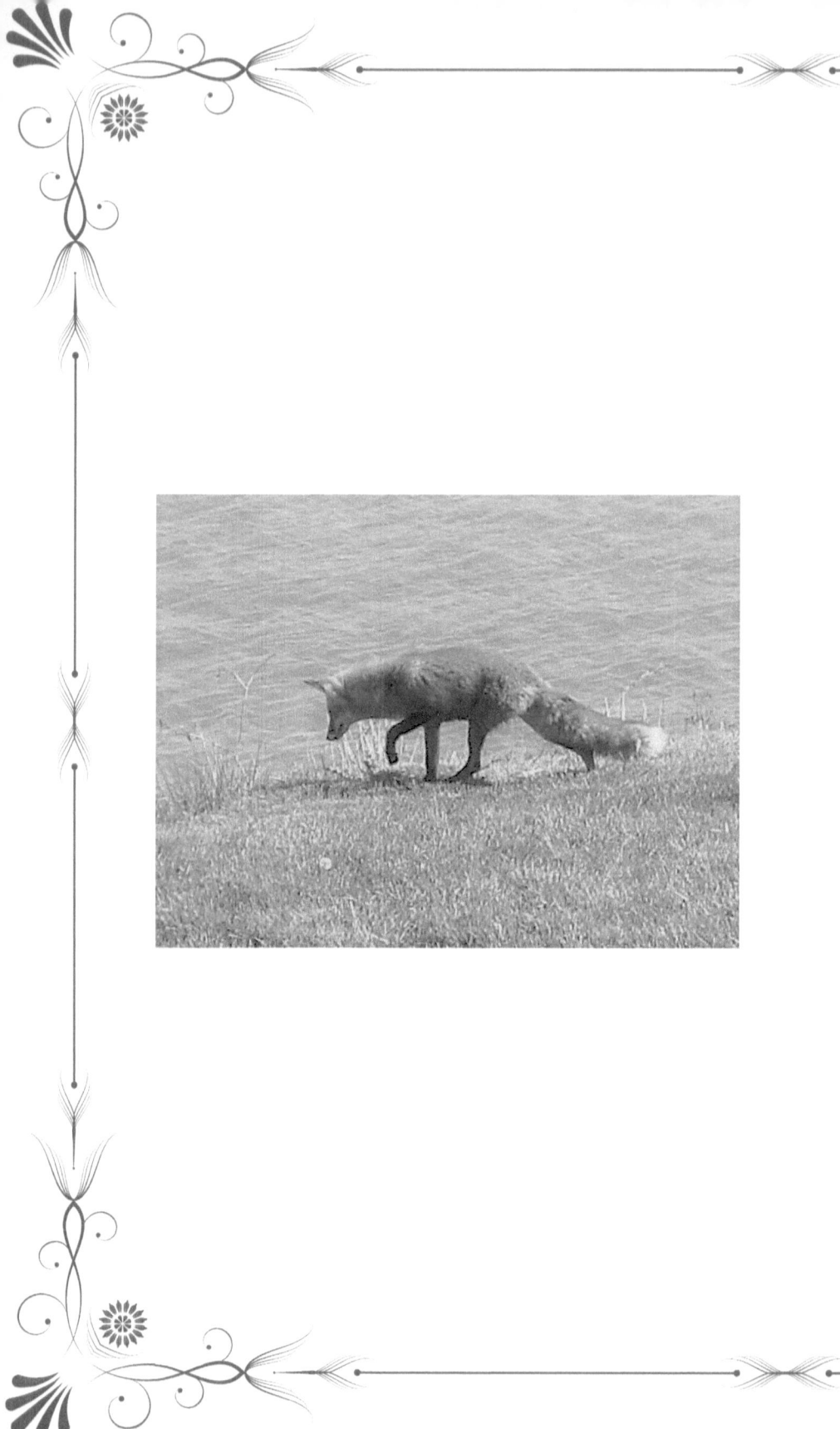

Fox and the Fence

On this sunlit summer morning
Watching butterflies and bees
Amid the festive wildflowers
And hillside green with trees
There appears before me
A fox so spry and lean
He's running around so madly
What is it he's seen?
And how is it he's here today?
My fenced in yard secure
I'll watch this action going on
Need some answers, that's for sure
Well, he's marking off this space for his.
Spraying tree and bush and fence,
I think he's warning others
This looks like there's suspense.
Now he's sprinting with great speed,
He leaps the high white fence.
It's almost, and he tries again.
His ego is immense!
But wait, he sniffs a small hole
Near the bottom of the fence.
Uh, oh, he's found the groundhog's door
And, boom, he follows scents.
At first he can't get through there.
This hole seems much too small.
But, cunning fox persists then gone!
And now, I've told you all.

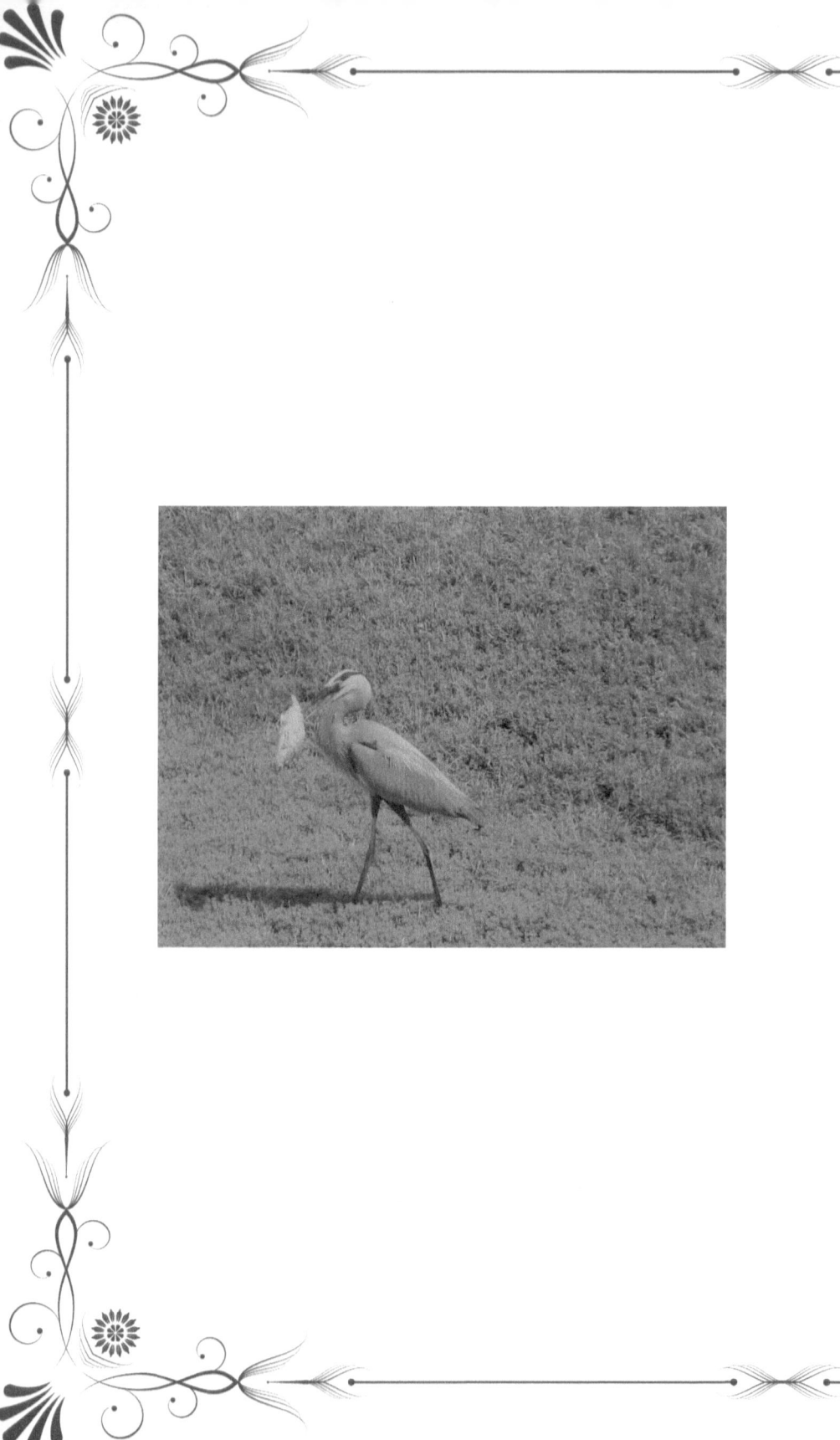

Great Blue Heron

Heron, with your long thin legs
I see you out there snacking
Along the edges of the pond
Your early flight impacting
It is so punctual
This I'll note
What is it in your flying?
Makes the other birds respond,
"It's grace mid air applying."
Perhaps it is your great size
With wing span five feet large
Perhaps it is your attitude
I'm here, and I'm in charge!
But this one thing is special
The birds around all sing
It's almost like they're greeting you,
"Behold, here comes our king!"

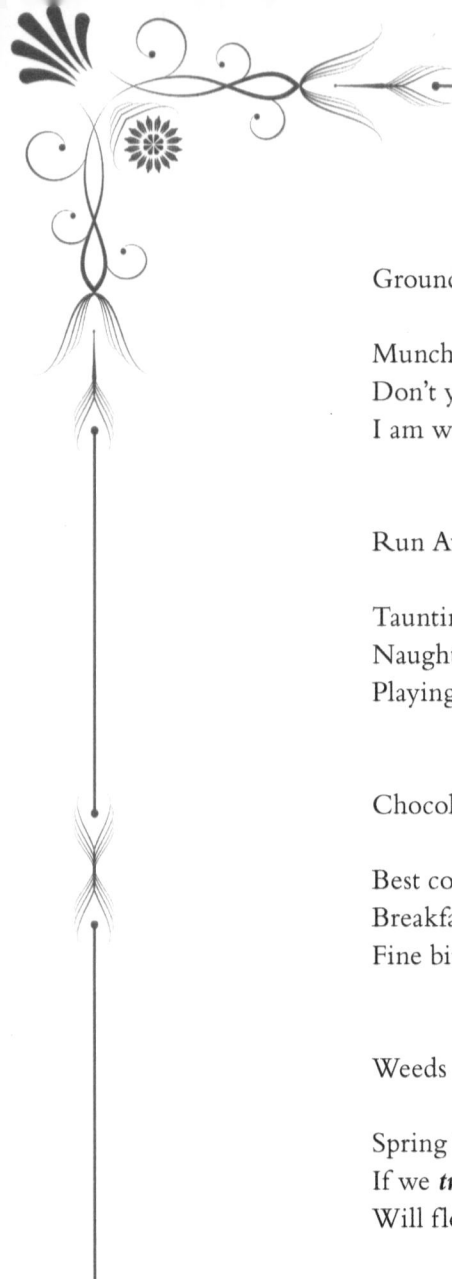

Haiku

Groundhog

Munching all day long
Don't you dare eat my new plants.
I am watching you!

Run Away Dog

Taunting your owner
Naughty, teasing smile so clear
Playing hide and seek.

Chocolates and Coffee

Best combination
Breakfast, lunch and dinner time,
Fine bitter-sweet treat.

Weeds

Spring battle begins
If we *try* to grow strong weeds
Will flowers gain strength?

Watching My Weight

Ounce by ounce it goes
Up and up and up again.
But, I'm watching it!

Trying to Sleep

Snuggled in covers
Sleepily relaxed and yet,
Where's brain off button?

Dental Hygienist

My satin smooth teeth
Make my tongue want to thank you,
Dental hygienist.

Grocery Shopping

The list is quite short
Why is my basket so full?
Empty stomach rules!

Saving Money

It starts out so young
Dimes go into the piggy!
Retirement's fine.

Eat Your Veggies

My mother was right
Every meal, eat some veggies.
Listen to your mom.

Gratitude

Appreciation
So joyful to express it
Thank you, thanks again.

Perseverance

When you fall, get up.
When you fail, do better next.
Repeat! Repeat! **YAY!**

Trust

Believe, have faith, care.
Confident expectation,
Reliable you.

Commitment

Pledge and bind to it
Others depend that you do
Just know that you will.

Courage

Heart with valor true
Bravery well respected
That stands for your life.

Loyalty

Faithful to ideals
Faithful to your own country
Faithfulness is you.

Integrity

Honesty, have it
Sincerity, a treasure
Hone it, and own it.

Service

A friendly action
Work done often for others
You're very helpful.

Character

Top reputation
A very distinctive trait
You have moral strength.

Dignity

Degree of honor
Worthiness with self respect
You earned high repute.

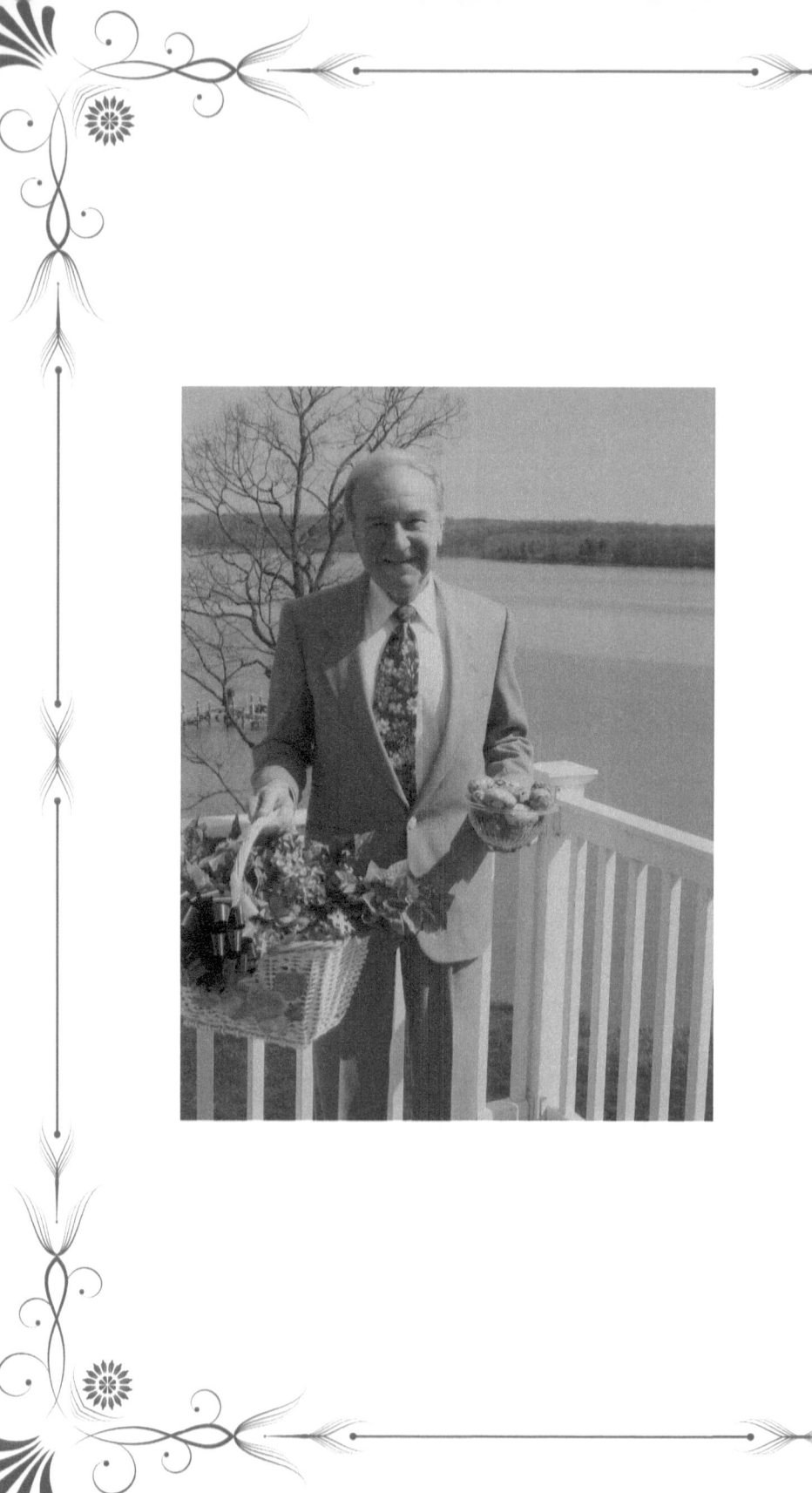

Happy Everything

My family lives so far away
It's often we will need to say,

"Happy Everything"

We toast to birthdays on the phone
By planes, cars, rails we tend to roam
E'en when we celebrate from home,

It's "Happy Everything"

It could be valentines with hearts
Or packages mailed with many tarts
How e're the celebrating starts,

For "Happy Everything"

Sometimes it's Easter when we meet
That is a very tender treat,

Yes, "Happy Everything"

Memorial Day's a special time
We honor Veterans, your and mine
Their sacrifices so divine!

"Happy Everything"

We love to join in Florida
Resorts and sunshine "galore-ida"
Palm trees, Disney "more-of-a"
Relax, drink, eat "smore-of-a"

"Happy Everything"

Thanksgiving, Christmas times to gather
Anniversaries, birthdays sometimes we blather,

"Happy Everything"

The main thing it's about is love
Enjoy these words that push and shove,

For "Happy Everything"

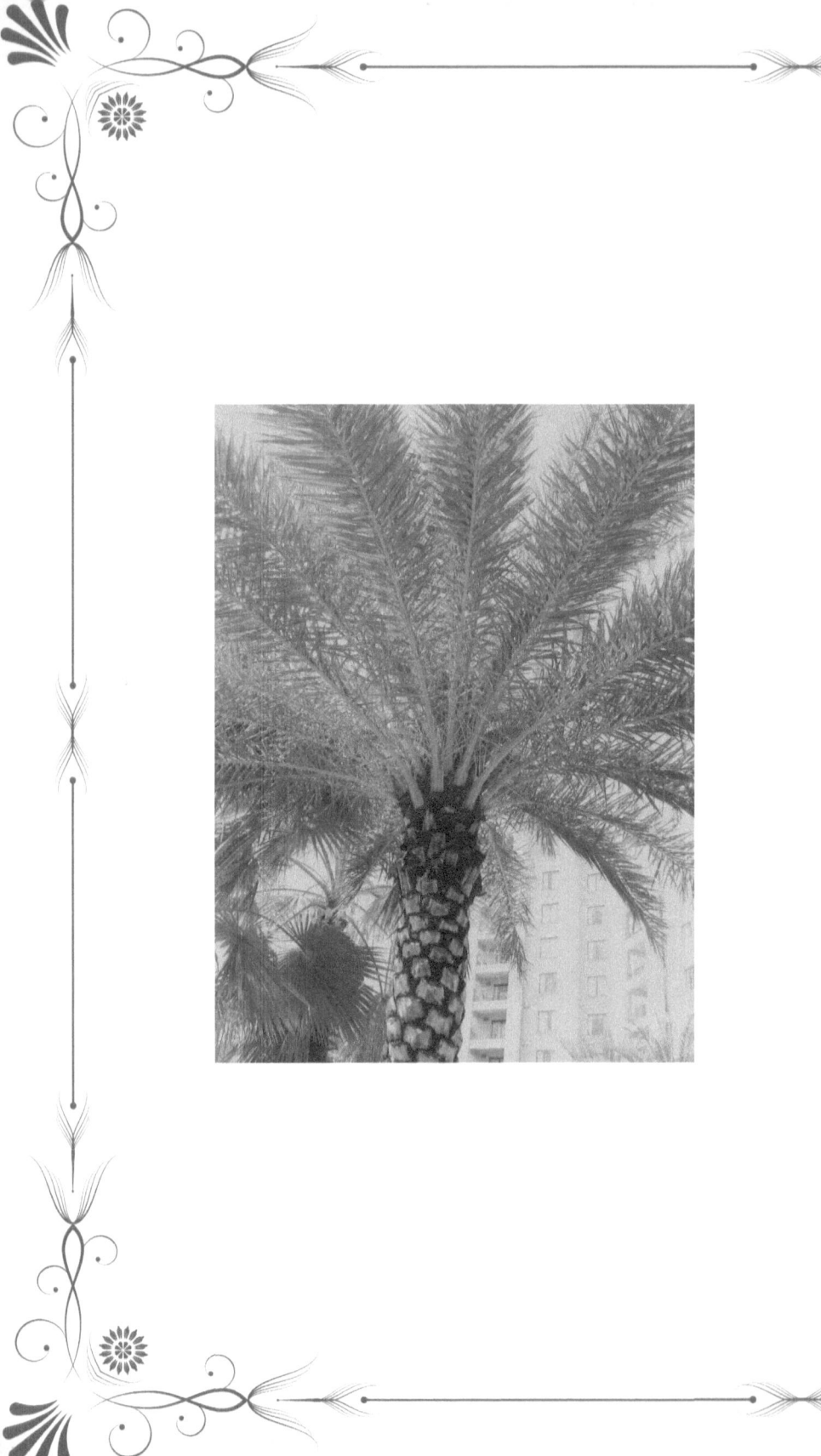

Help! Help!

Written in 2020
During the COVID-19
Pandemic

I need to go somewhere
I need to do something new

Like a caged bird
I yearn to fly away

We try to be careful
We try to stay safe

But, being trapped inside
Not seeing family
Not seeing friends

Is making me

```
    R
C   a   Y
    Z
```

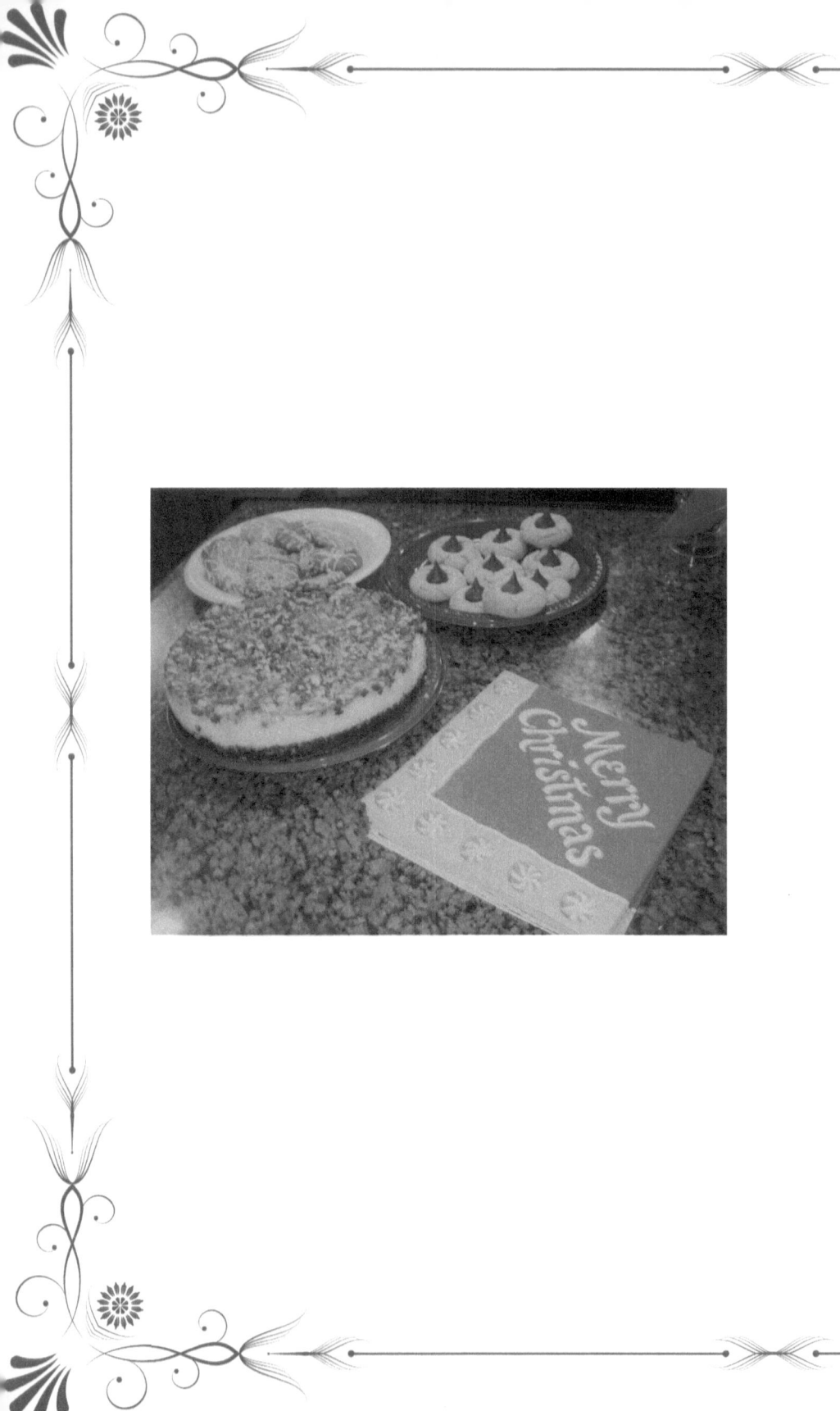

High Heels in the Sand

Yes, I saw this
Really saw this
As stupid as it sounds,
A lady wearing high heels,
Walking in the sand.
She didn't try to take them off
And walk in barefoot mode
But, lurched and staggered
Onward bound---
Wearing high heels in the sand.
At first I wondered,
"Is she drunk?"
"Or is the sand too hot?"
But, no, it was a coolish day,
And sexy, it was not!

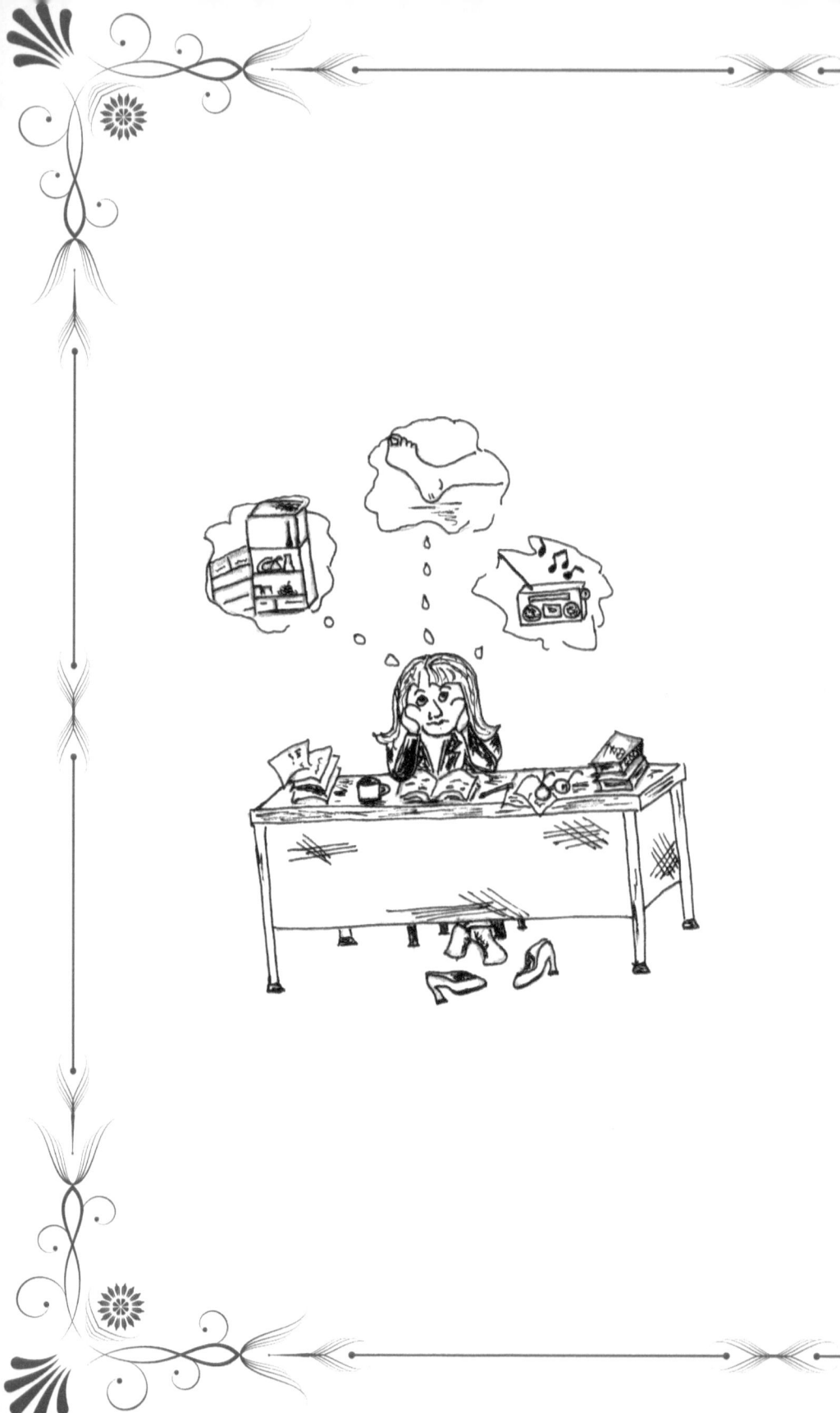

I Need to Study

I need to study 'cuz tests are near
My up pop toaster body dear
Won't stay put to read each page
My mind, it wants to disengage!

I know a magnet's
In my tum
It pulls me to the frig, yum, yum,
And I just have to bush my hair
And hem up my new underwear.

My toenails look a bit too long,
I have to hear just one more song.

Oops, how could it now be so late?
I'll study on another date...
And then ---

I'll not procrastinate!

Idaho Heart

'Twas luck to be born in Idaho
Where the sun rises o'er the peaks
Where neighbors know and care about folks
And the pioneer spirit's not meek.

In my Idaho heart I feel the grandeur
Of the river of no return
The mighty Salmon River will set you straight
When you think you've no more to learn.

Famous Idaho potatoes and huckleberry pie
Fresh salmon and rainbow trout
Venison stew from a hunting adventure
And T-bone steaks to tout.

I can smell the pine forests and the damp rich earth
In the center of my mind
As I sit in DC I yearn to go back
To the peace I know I'll find.

In my travels all over, South America, Rome,
Hawaii to Saint Thomas Island
Paris, France and Boston, Mass
It's Idaho to me that's grand.

Famous Idaho potatoes and huckleberry pie
Fresh salmon and rainbow trout
Venison stew from a hunting adventure
And T-bone steaks to tout.

For in Idaho the culture's diverse
With Basque and the Indian tribes
Irish, Scots, Chinese, Czechs
Japanese and Hispanics abide.
Golden wheat fields always waved at me

Driving north to school I'd find
Friendly farmhouses among the rolling hills
In the silos of my mind.

My Idaho heart grew up with love,
Family, community, and friends,
Ice cream socials, pot luck dinners at church
Singing songs that never end.

So dear Idaho, I want you to know
You're calling me to roam
As my Idaho heart hears songs in the wind
'Round the campfires near my home.

Famous Idaho potatoes and huckleberry pie
Fresh salmon and rainbow trout
Venison stew from a hunting adventure
And T-bone steaks to tout.

I'm a Septuagenarian

I'm a septuagenarian
Was once a librarian
I've lived a long life, that's true.
Now I've joined the Aquarium
It's super splendarium,
There's always something to do.

I'm Nuts About Nuts

I'm nuts
I'm nuts
I'm nuts about nuts

We're nuts
We're nuts
We're nuts about nuts.

We eat almonds on our cereal
Peanut butter on our toast
Pecans in our ice cream
Cashews when I am the host.

Walnuts
Pecans
Hazelnuts
Pistachios
Brazils
Cashews
Peanuts

Brazils have selenium
Walnuts with omega 3's
Peanuts have a lot of zinc
Almond milk is great to drink
Add some chocolate
Helps you think.

Hazelnut coffee
Nuts in crackers
Nuts in shells
Peanuts and baseball
Mixed nuts taste swell

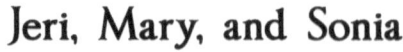

Jeri, Mary, and Sonia

A beautiful,
A healthy boy,
This baby sent by God
To be so loved
To bring great joy
To these strong mothers three.

Each mom had a special role
To fulfill this plan,
So complex yet spiritual,
Baby into man.

Nine months nurtured
Nine months belong
Infused with love and hope
From beginning
Mother's love strong
Each one with heart of gold.

Love unending and divine
Sent from God on high,
Mysterious, sweet and kind
Hearts together tie.

Happy Birthday to you, David
From your poet aunt, Aunt Linda

September 29, 2018

Jeri

A poem for you by your sister, Linda Glod

My sister's an angel
I can just see her now
Remodeling heaven
She'll be showing them how.

A beautiful angel
With a heart made of gold
Her hair shining copper
And a will of steel, bold.

In time for Dad's birthday,
Yes, it's her birthday, too,
Celebrating together
Like they once used to do.

Our mother will be there
With relatives and friends
Heav'n has a new angel,
And there, joy never ends.

My dear sister, Jeri,
Friend, confidante, sincere,
A loving, smart, mentor,
Having courage, not fear.

A great sense of humor
Always willing to share,
So ready to comfort
Showing others you care.

Fifty one years of marriage
To Bruce, brother-in-law, kind,
Gave us Katherine and family
With Stephanie's crew, we all bind.

What blessings they all are,
We share memories galore,
Plus family reunions—
Thanks! You organized more!

How you loved the vacations
The adventures, the zing,
Remember "Tower of Terror"?
What a thrill that thought brings.

Your siblings all miss you
Now a hole in each life,
There's Joann, Don, and Linda,
Add their husbands and wife.

"A fun aunt," Aunt Jeri,
My children adored her,
A sister-in-law special,
My husband described her.

Crank up music in heaven
More pianos to hear,
A talented musician
Playing "Polonaise", cheer.

Sing "Zip-a-dee-doo-dah",
Add sunflowers bright,
Then look up to heaven
You'll see one more bright light.

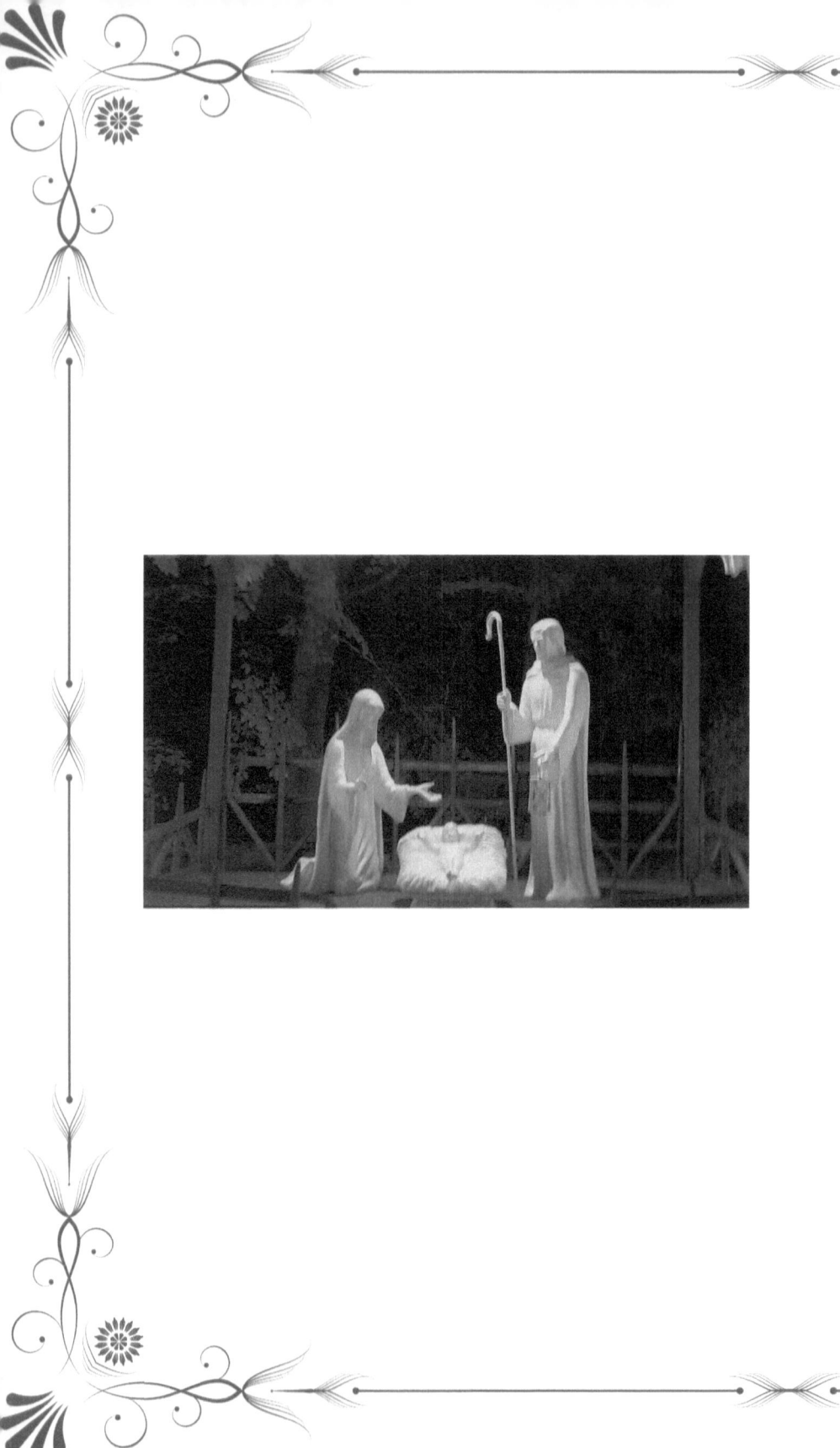

Jesus

Lyrics

Jesus
When I wake up
Today will be special
Jesus
When I make coffee
Great things await me
Jesus
As I prepare breakfast
I feel excitement
Jesus
As I look out the window
A beautiful world awakens
Jesus
Your love engulfs me
You protect me
Jesus
You gave me life
You gave me strength
Jesus
You gave me gifts
I must use them for You
Jesus
Today is for You
Each day is for You
Jesus
I'll share the joy
I'll share your love
Jesus
You fill my heart
You fill my soul
Jesus

A Limerick for Adrienne

ADRIENNE GIGGLES AND COOS,

THEN CLOSES HER EYES FOR A SNOOZE.

SHE SMILES AT HER MOTHER,

NEXT DADDY AND BROTHER,

DEAR GRANDDAUGHTER, ADRIENNE'S, OUR MUSE!

For Brianna

A LIMERICK

BRIANNA HAS BEAUTY AND SMARTS,

SHE'S DEFINITELY STRONG
IN OUR HEARTS,

A COMPOSER, FOR SURE,

LIKE CHOPIN, SHE'LL ENDURE.

DEAR GRANDDAUGHTER,
YOU'LL TOP THE CHARTS!

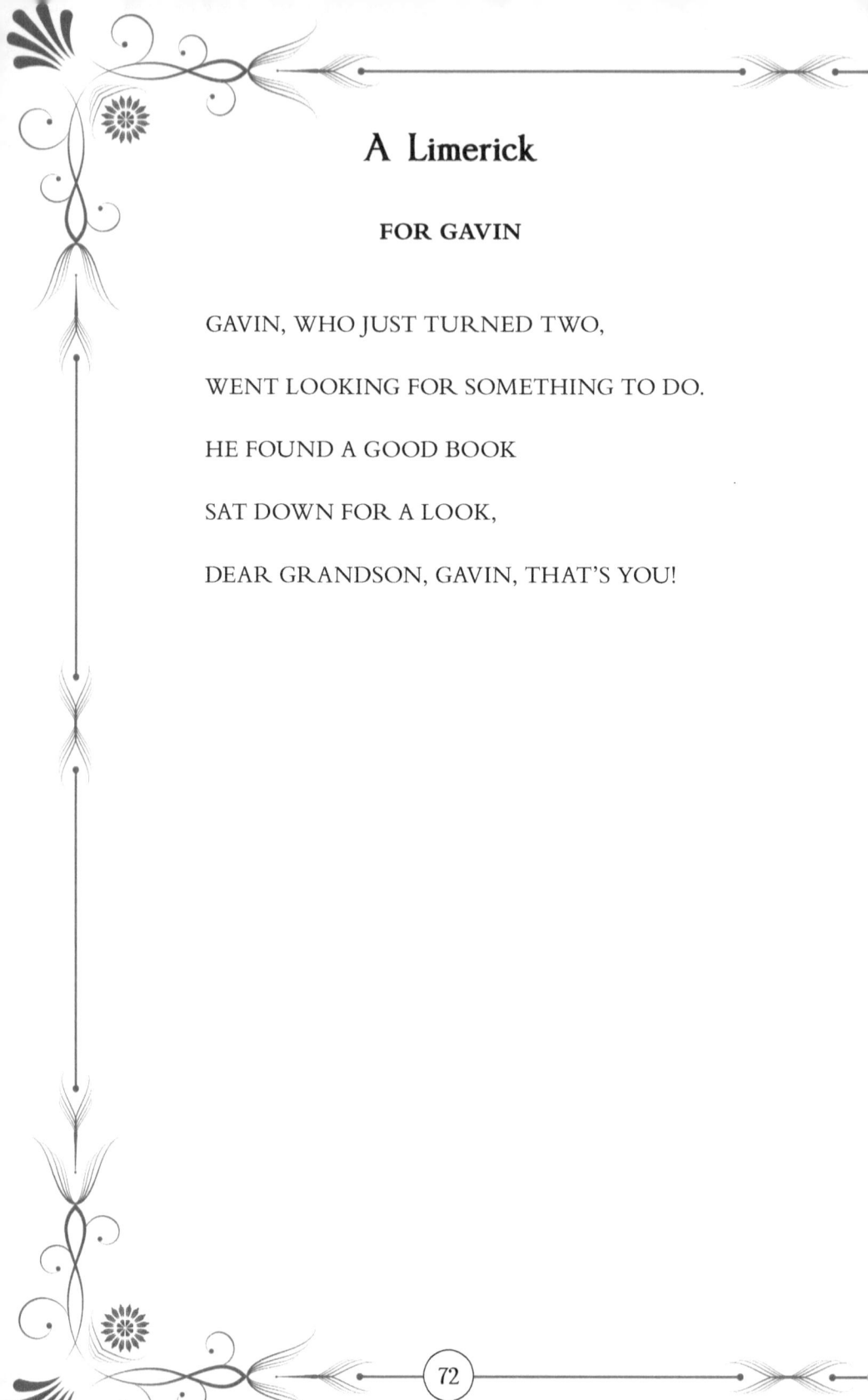

A Limerick

FOR GAVIN

GAVIN, WHO JUST TURNED TWO,

WENT LOOKING FOR SOMETHING TO DO.

HE FOUND A GOOD BOOK

SAT DOWN FOR A LOOK,

DEAR GRANDSON, GAVIN, THAT'S YOU!

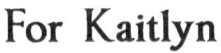

For Kaitlyn

THERE IS A SMART GIRL
NAMED KAITLYN,

WHO LOVES TO TWIRL IN HER criNOLINE.

SHE GIGGLES AND LAUGHS

WHILE SPINNING HER CALVES,

OUR GRANDDAUGHTER DEAR,
THAT'S KAITLYN!

A Limerick for Natalie

NATALIE'S PRETTY AND BRIGHT.

SHE'S A JOY, WE LOVE,
THAT'S RIGHT.

CARTOONS SHE CAN DRAW

THAT PUTS US IN AH,

DEAR GRANDDAUGHTER,
YOU'VE GOT THE MIGHT!

For Ryan

A limerick

THERE IS A BRIGHT BOY NAMED RYAN,

WHO LIKES TO ROAR LIKE A LION

AND SMILES SO WIDE

BIG SIS BY HIS SIDE,

OUR GRANDSON, SO DEAR, THAT'S RYAN.

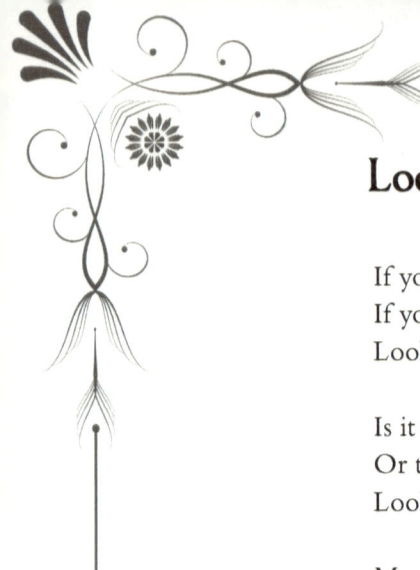

Look on the Chair

If you can't find it here
If you can't find it there
Look on the chair!

Is it the blue shirt?
Or the T shirt?
Look on the chair.

Maybe the red socks
Or the white socks
Look on the chair.

Your orange sweatshirt?
"Yes!" I'll now blurt,
"Look on the chair!!"

I'm seeing black belts
Even some fur pelts
Under the chair.

There's your striped tie
And your tie dye,
Behind the chair.

So, don't stand and stare
You'll find it there
"Cuz, it's on the chair!

Middle School Peacocks

Middle school peacocks
In plumes of hair
Strutting to school
While others stare.
Fixing clothes
So labels show
In talking, screeching packs they go.
Inward fears
They'll hide in vain—
Can't pass mirrors
Nor windowpanes,
Phones past four
Won't be the same!
Energy explodes within
Wanting to cry,
Then next, to grin.
How long is this peacock stage?
And what's in store
At the next stage?

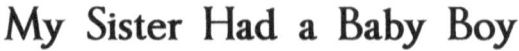

My Sister Had a Baby Boy

My sister had a baby boy
As precious as could be
She loved him with her heart and soul,
But, here is destiny.

She wasn't married at the time
It was a different age
She nurtured him inside her womb,
And this will set the stage.

She gave birth to her loving son
Not able to raise him then
My sister prayed that God would have
A love filled home for him.

Her prayers were answered on that day
A loving family waited
They would raise this baby boy
And they were so elated.

My sister loved him all her life
Her prayers were strong for him
She stayed connected in her heart
Sealed documents though win.

While she was living out her life
Her baby boy grew strong
The sealed records of his birth
Were sealed away too long.

Her baby grew into a man
With wisdom, strength, and love,
His angel watched him night and day
God sheltered from above.

Then came the time when it could be
The records were unsealed
What was this secret long ago?
This mystery revealed.

He found his mother, yes indeed
The one who gave him life
But she had gone to heaven now,
And he had found his wife.

The beauty of this story
Is very plain to see
The unborn child is precious
Proclaim its dignity.

I'll meet him Monday morning
My nephew and my friend
We'll praise God for his mother
The unborn we'll defend!

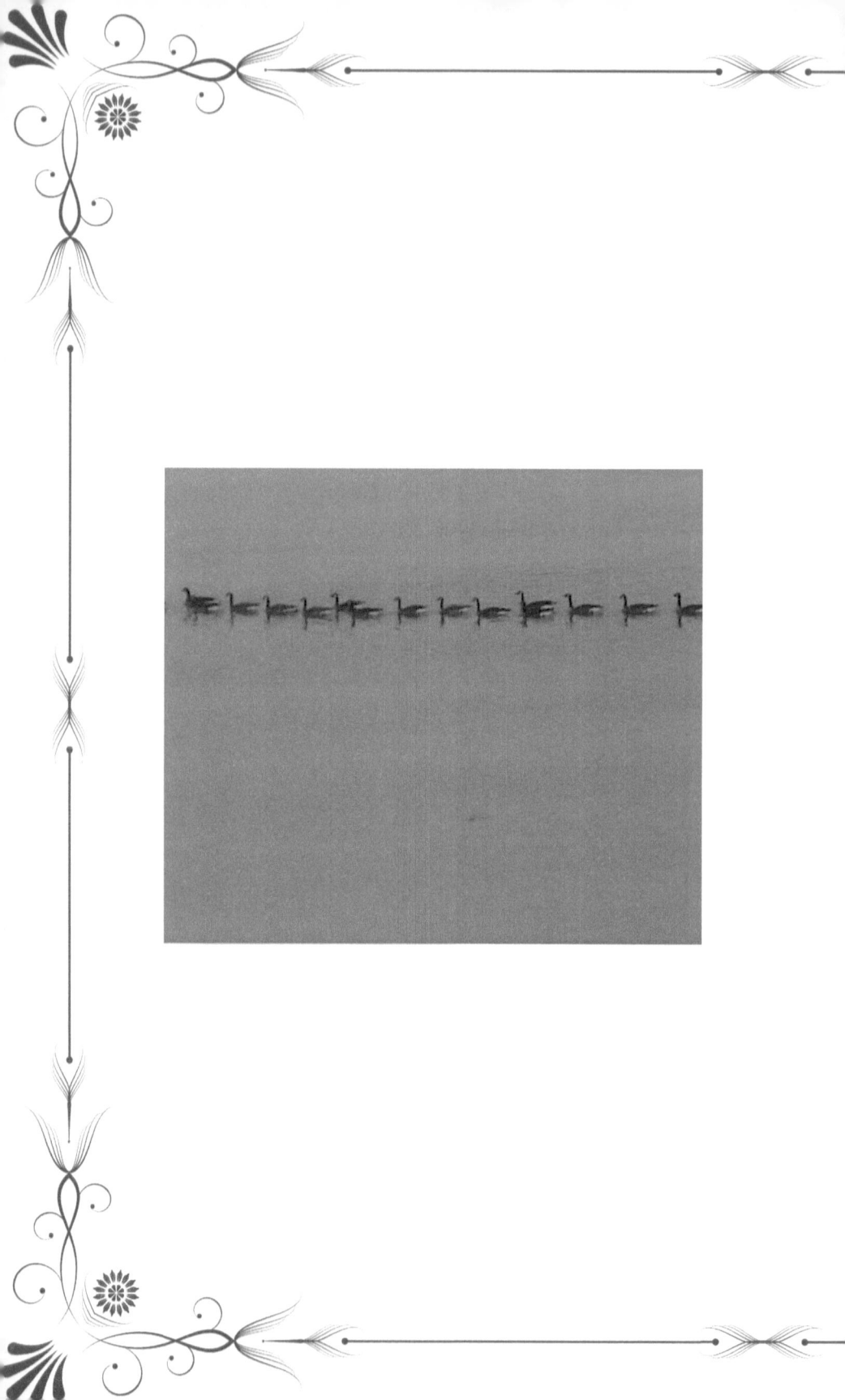

Perfect

Ocean waves lapping the beach
In perfect rhythm,
Geese flying over the waves
Perfect formation,
Sun setting quietly now
In perfect timing,
God pouring love out to you
His perfect planning,
Listen, He's calling to you
You're perfect for Him,
Knowing you before you're born
In perfect timing,
Your talents are needed now
Perfect formation,
God's love is blessing us all
His perfect planning!

Praying Mantis

Praying for
a juicy bug
a companion
a sunny day
inspirational
keeping form
no movement
focused
intent
determined
alert
fearless
duty bound
big job to do
masterful
friend to man
always welcome here
please return
anytime.

Praying Mantis poem was inspired by this fascinating creature sitting so prominently
on our lawn chair doing his job.

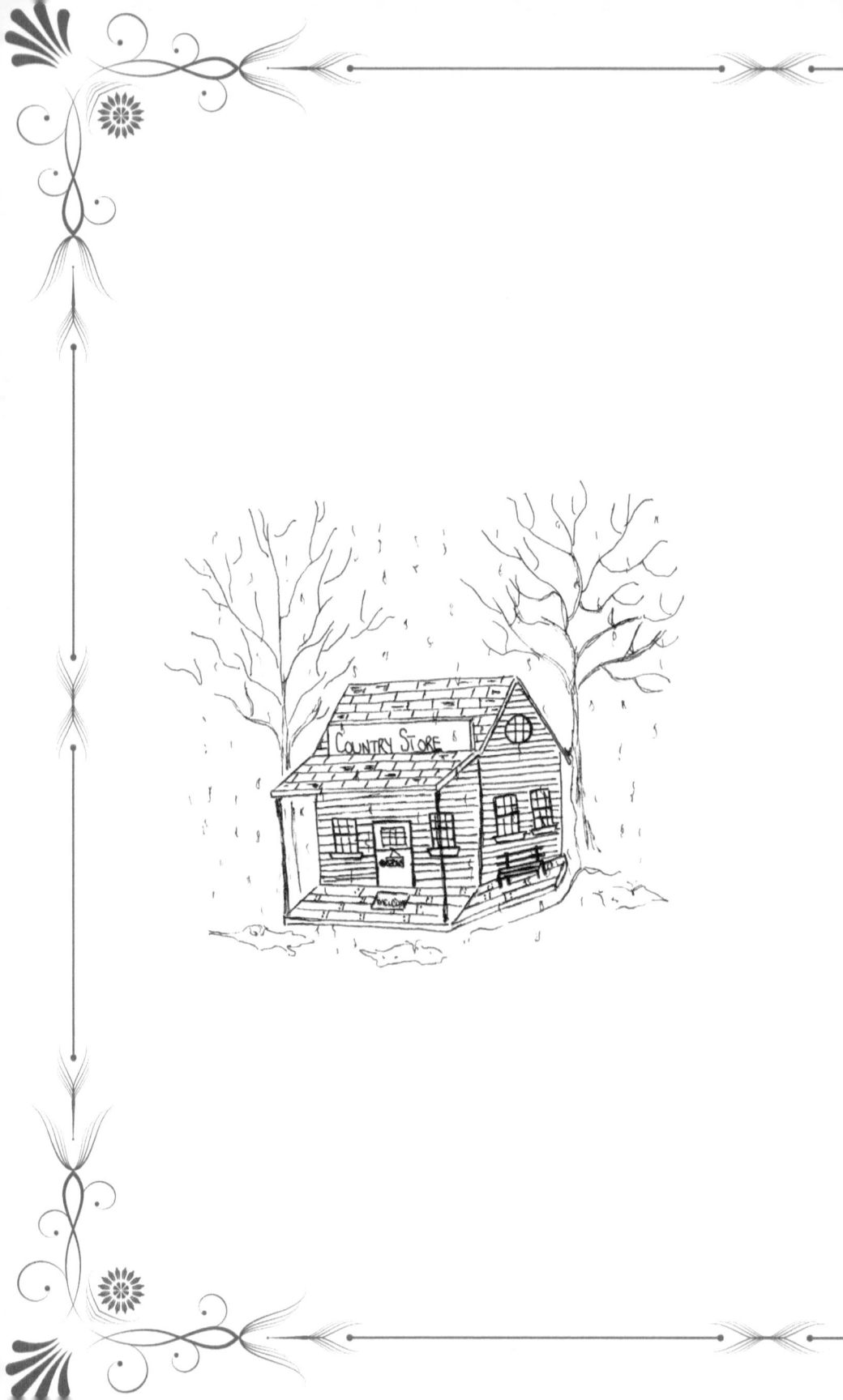

Rain and Country Stores

Rained out of beach plans
So it was
That country stores filled in,
What treasures we discovered
In woods, in lace, and tin.
The candle scented shops
Were so stuffed full
Of wondrous art,
Each piece
A special just so cut
With tender painted hearts,
Some spread
In zesty colored hues
To catch the eye of art.
Then hunger told us
Time to eat
So, country food we found.
Each simple dish
A tasty treat
Our talking did abound.
We talked of dreams
We talked of life
As raindrops
Hit the ground.

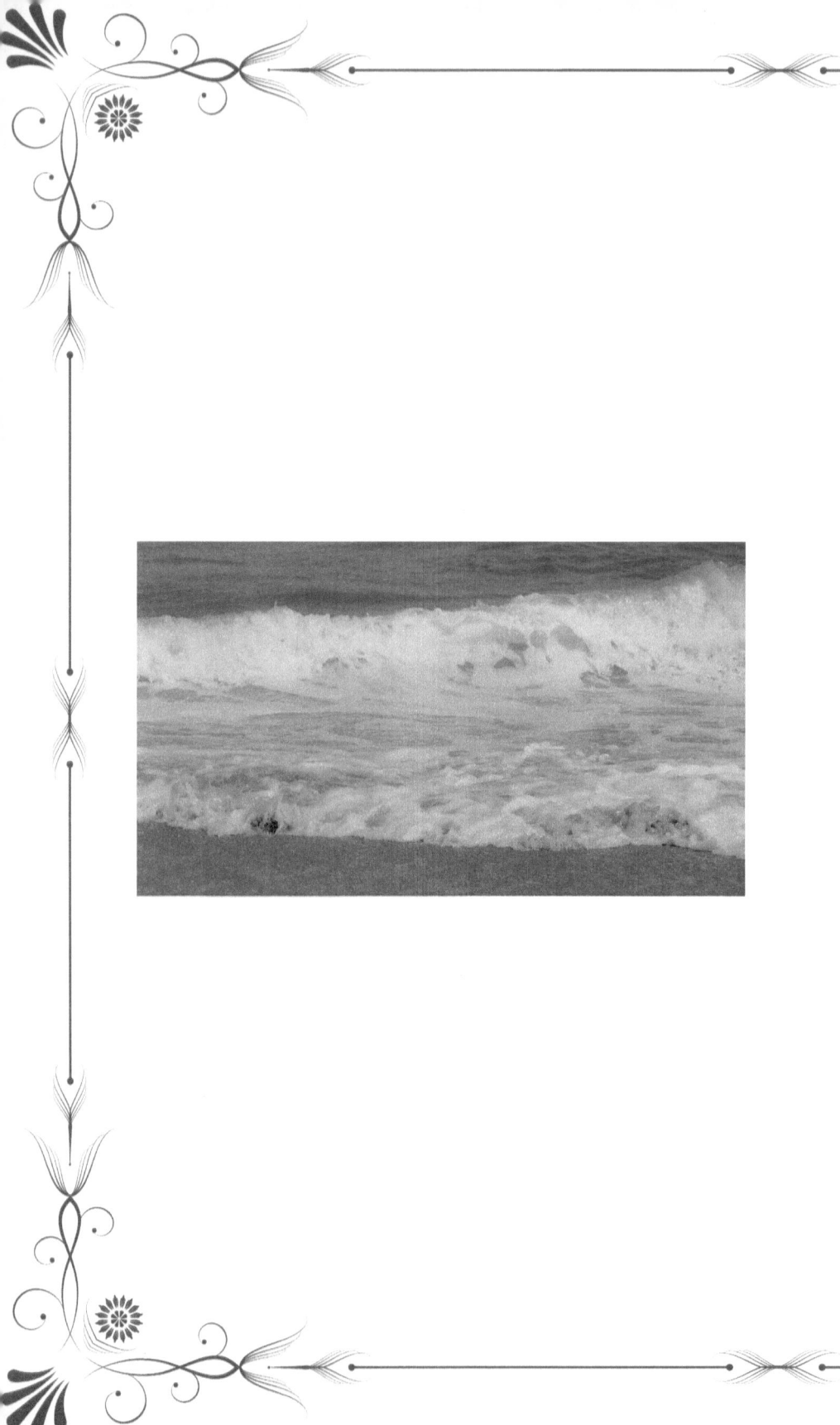

Red Beads

Five a. m.
Red Beads
So tightly strung
Glow in the early darkness
Moving in precision
At the tilt of a curve
An upward hill
All proceed in determined order.
Yellow oversized platter moon
Decorates the scene
Low hanging
Just above
The red beads
So tightly strung.

Driving from Quantico, Virginia north on 95 at 5 a.m. on March 19, 2019

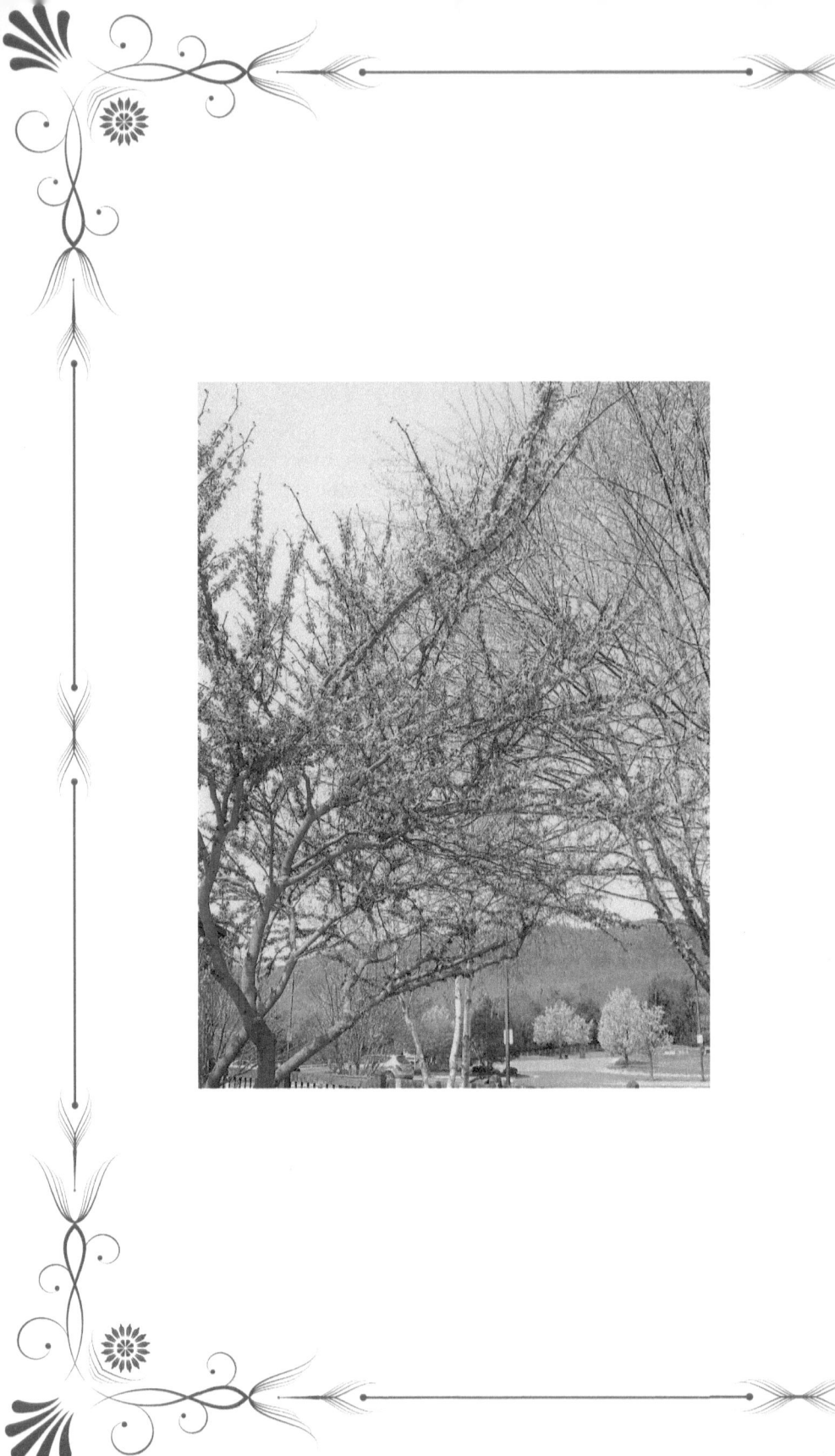

The Kiss of Spring

Invigorated by the warm sun's hug,
The kiss of spring rejoices
After Arctic wind blasts cease,
And a calming breeze
Takes charge.

Tender pink blossoms
Highlight the sky blue scene,
Where birds sing mightily,
Cheering all who hear
The new sounds
Of the season.

Forsythia so fashionably
Dressed in bright yellow,
Boasts a "look at me"
Attitude as she waves,
In spring's calming breeze.

Ruby red tulips
Stand at attention,
Honoring spring's arrival!

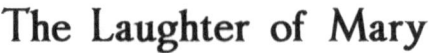

The Laughter of Mary

The laughter of Mary
Still rings in my heart
From her joyful spirit
We'll never depart.
So caring and loving
To my brother, Don,
They bonded forever
On earth and beyond
Two beautiful babies,
One Steve and one Bill,
A most handsome family
Sweet dreams to fulfill.
She cherished her family
As did they in return
What wonderful memories
Life's lessons we learn.
We love you, dear Mary,
For you, yes, we yearn.

Rest in Peace
October 15, 2020

Written with love
Honoring
Mary Charlotte Snook Scott

Thinking of you

Thankful for you
Hope all is well
In our prayers always
Naturally kind you
Know that you are missed
I hope to see you soon
Happy thoughts of you
Great memories we share

Ocean breezes make me think of you
Forever friend

Yes, you are the best!
Oh, when will you come and visit?
United in love and friendship

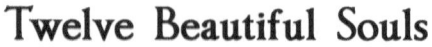

Twelve Beautiful Souls

A Memorial Poem

You'll never know the time or place.
On May 31, that was the case.
Twelve beautiful souls were taken to heaven.

What can we learn from their hopes and dreams?
What will we do as each memory gleams?
Twelve beautiful souls were taken to heaven.

Each had gifts and talents strong.
How could a day of living go so wrong?
Twelve beautiful souls were taken to heaven.

Their loving families and special friends
Knitted together as eternity mends
Twelve beautiful souls were taken to heaven.

Bless Christopher, Robert and Herbert,
Bless Katherine, Mary, and Gayle,
Bless Joshua, Laquita, and Michelle,
Bless Ryan, Richard, and Alexander.

Twelve Beautiful Souls Were Taken to Heaven.

A part of each of us died with you that day.
Good-bys are so very hard to say.
Twelve beautiful souls were taken to heaven.

May you rest in peace.

Twilight Frog

Hi, cutie,
You're back, I see!
This is now a thing
Between you and me.

There you are
All dressed in green,
The most striking shade
That I've ever seen.

Those big eyes
So round, so bright,
I'm wondering now,
This frog at twilight.

Handsome prince,
Who needs a kiss!
Unlock the magic
From your special miss.

Twilight frog,
Go door to the right,
You have the wrong house,
My Prince is my Light.

(Or, have an alternate last line which is)
My prince is my knight.

This poem was inspired by a darling little frog that appeared each evening
on our patio glass door at Virginia Beach, peering in on us as we read or
watched TV.

Two Deer and the Fox

There they were feasting
Contented and free
Along came the fox
And said, "Look at me!"
The two does stood tall
Did not run from fright
Instead an action
Caused my delight.
Well, the next moment
Red fox had to run
With does chasing him
Now they're having fun.

Verbalize

A poem about taking action against cancer

Focus fight

Love learn laugh

Battle believe

Comfort cry

Celebrate

Wonder worry

Wait

Share snuggle sleep

Thank teach

Nourish notice

Offer observe

Encourage explore

Reminisce

Bond build

Dream discard

Give get

Sob smile

Listen

Compliment

Eliminate

Hope hug

Forgive forget

Giggle grin grow

Talk trust

Revisit

Savor sing

Call connect

Praise pray

Tease

Remember

Struggle

Hydrate

Patch plan

Reach release

Indulge

Sweeten

Dare do

Question

Yearn

Reconnect rejoice

Live

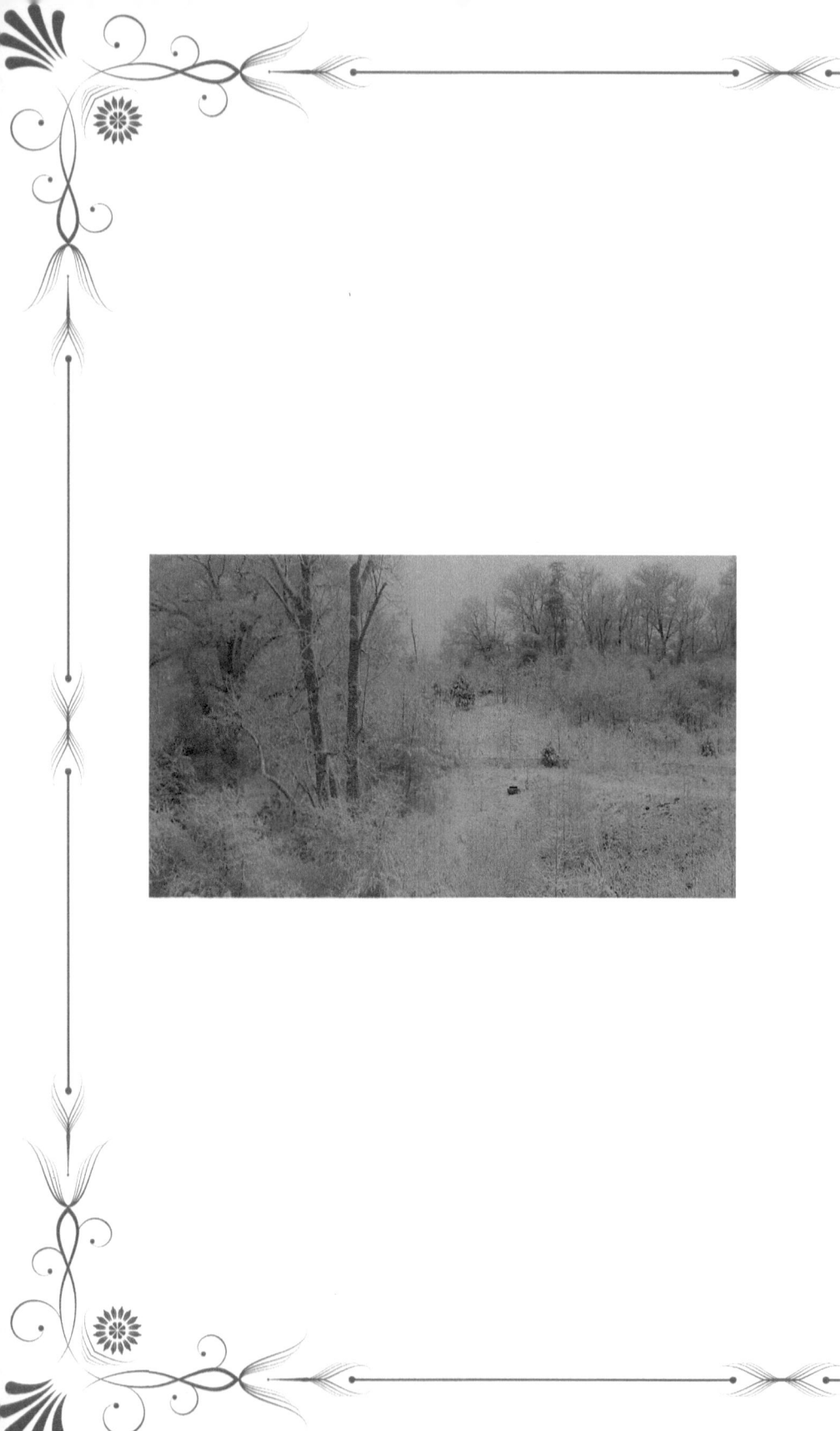

Virginia Limerick

Overnight all became white
Sidewalks and road are a fright
In three days it's over
Robins hopping in clover
In Virginia they do seasons right.

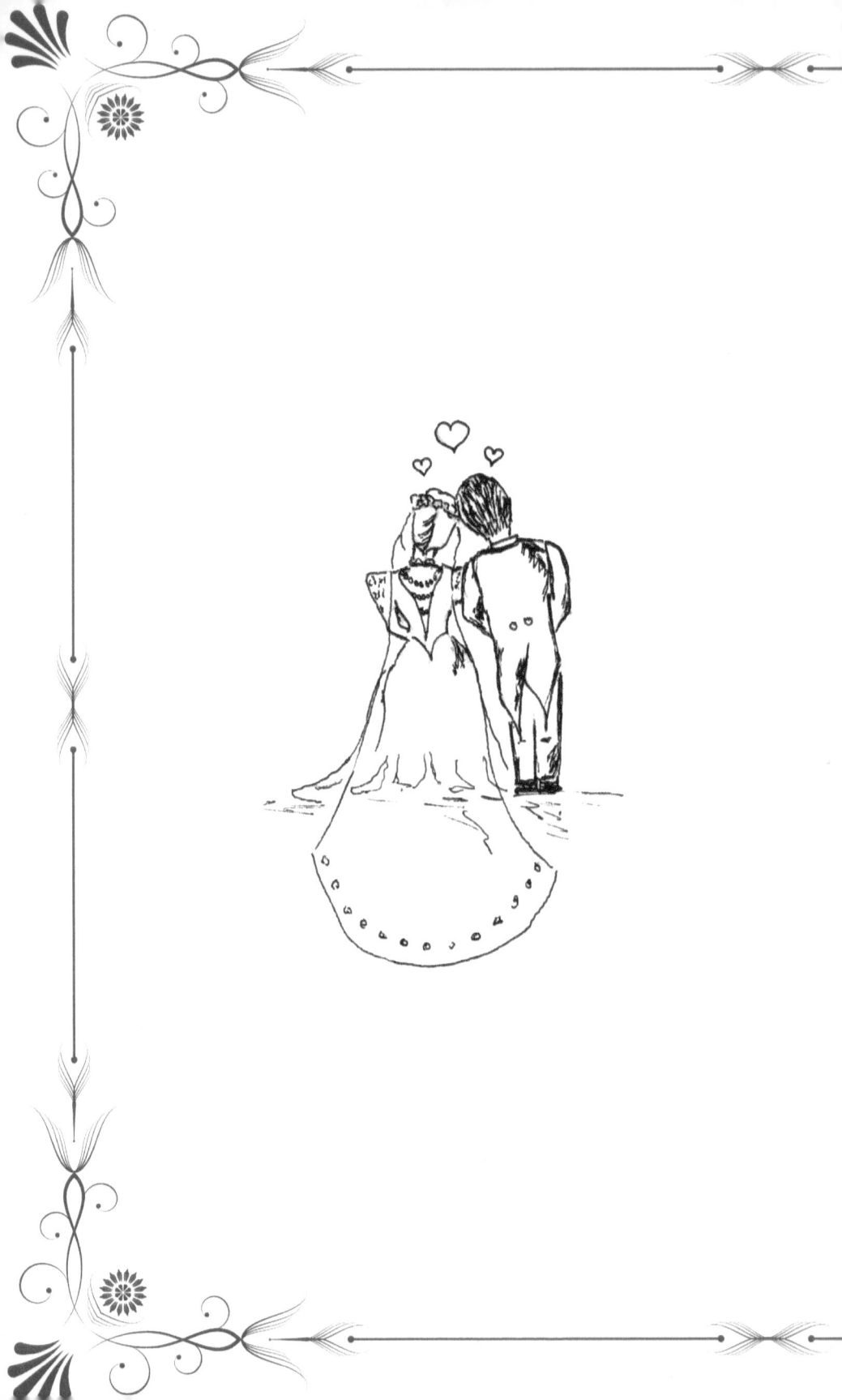

Wedding Song

I've waited so long
Knowing I'd find you out there,
It feels like a lifetime
Of holding this dream in place.

The power of true love
That magical mystery,
This once in a lifetime
Love, so rare, so pure.

Our spirits connected
The moment our eyes met
Our prayers fully answered,
My love, I found you.

I've waited so long
Knowing I'd find you out there
It feels like a lifetime
Of holding this dream in place.

I'll cherish you always.
I'll cherish this moment,
I'll honor and love you
My darling, now we're one.

We're stronger together,
Facing life as a team.
In good times and bad times
Our laughter will see us through.

I've waited so long
Knowing I'd find you out there,
It feels like a lifetimes
Of holding this dream in place.

My heart found its heaven.
My head found its earth.
We'll go forth together,
On our wedding day.

In sickness and sorrow
I'll be by your side.
We'll deal with life's troubles
With strength, by you side.

Our love grows much stronger
With each passing day.
I'll cherish you darling
During work time and play.

I've waited so long
Knowing I'd find you out there,
Patience rewarded,
We're putting our dream in place.

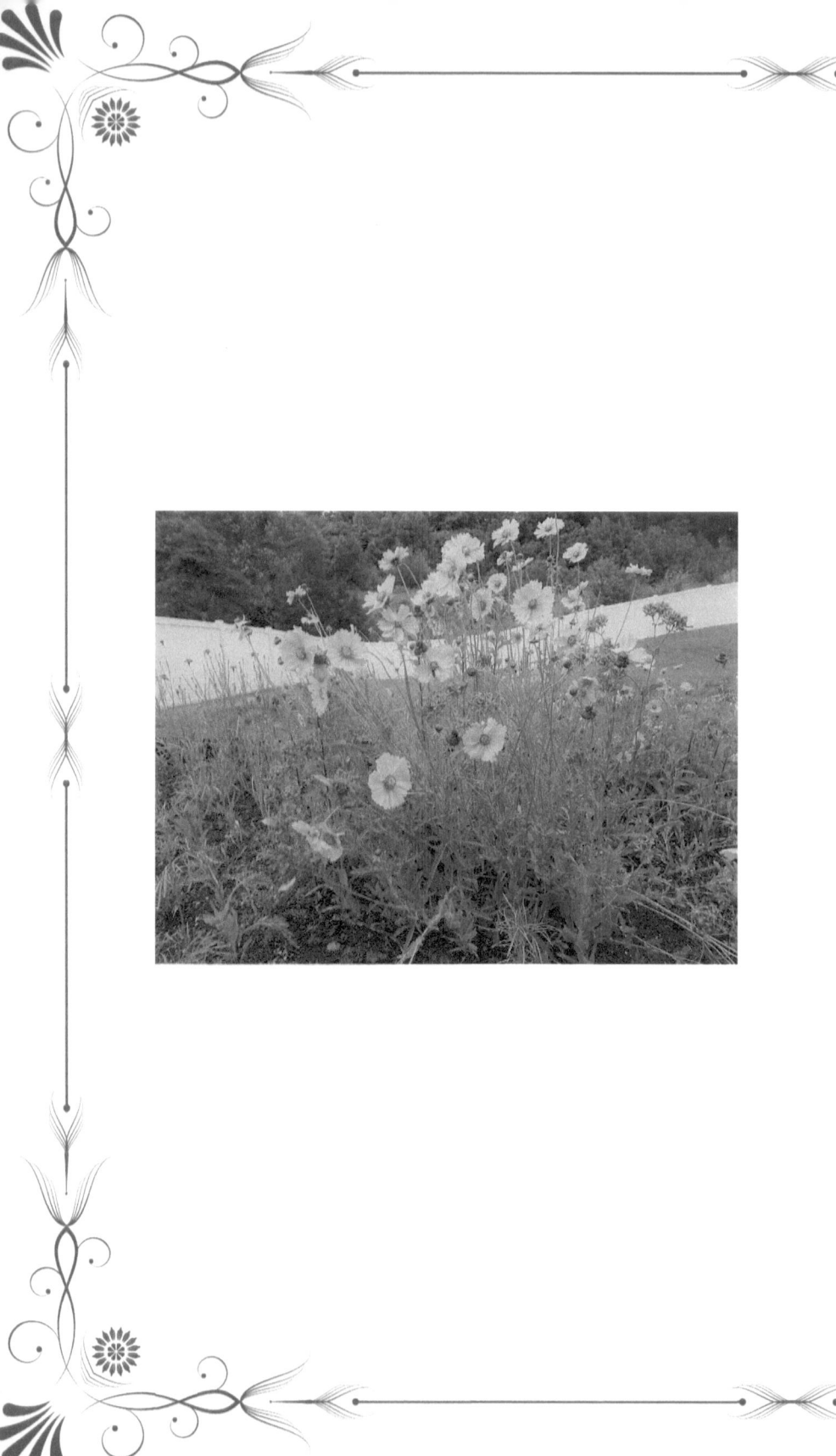

Wildflower Garden

I planted a wildflower garden here
It's bright and cheerful to see
My yard is a favorite hangout now,
For a wild canary.
He's a colorful bird
Of such miniature size
And so yellow as yellow can be
Now let's emphasize
As he's singing his song
A generous bird is he.
He just invited his family and friends
They flew out from all the trees
To come and enjoy his smorgasbord
What a wonderful sight to see.

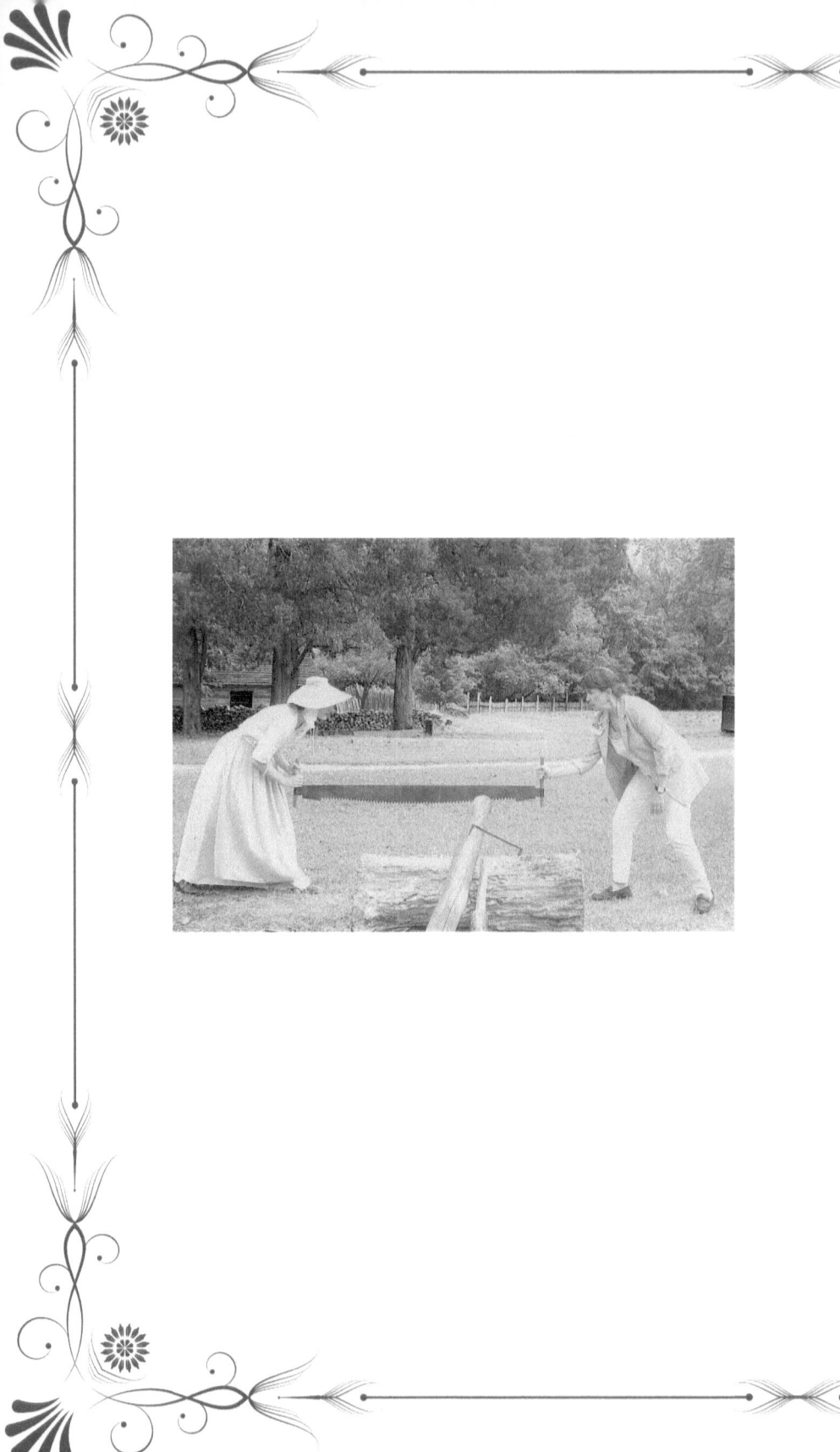

Work Work Work

Work, work, work
Sometimes we love it!
Sometimes we hate it!

Are you using your talents and skills?
Or are you working to just pay the bills?

There's a God spark within you
It's made for your view.

Work, work, work
Sometimes we love it!
Sometimes we hate it!

Yes, a message to play in your mind
That's one thing that makes God so kind

Listen and listen
Listen and then

Work, work, work
Sometimes we love it!
Sometimes we hate it!

In your soul on this day
With no time to delay

Discover that spark
It's your heart's mark
And shows the goodness of you
Ask God what he wants you to do

Work, work, work
Sometimes we love it!
Sometimes we hate it!

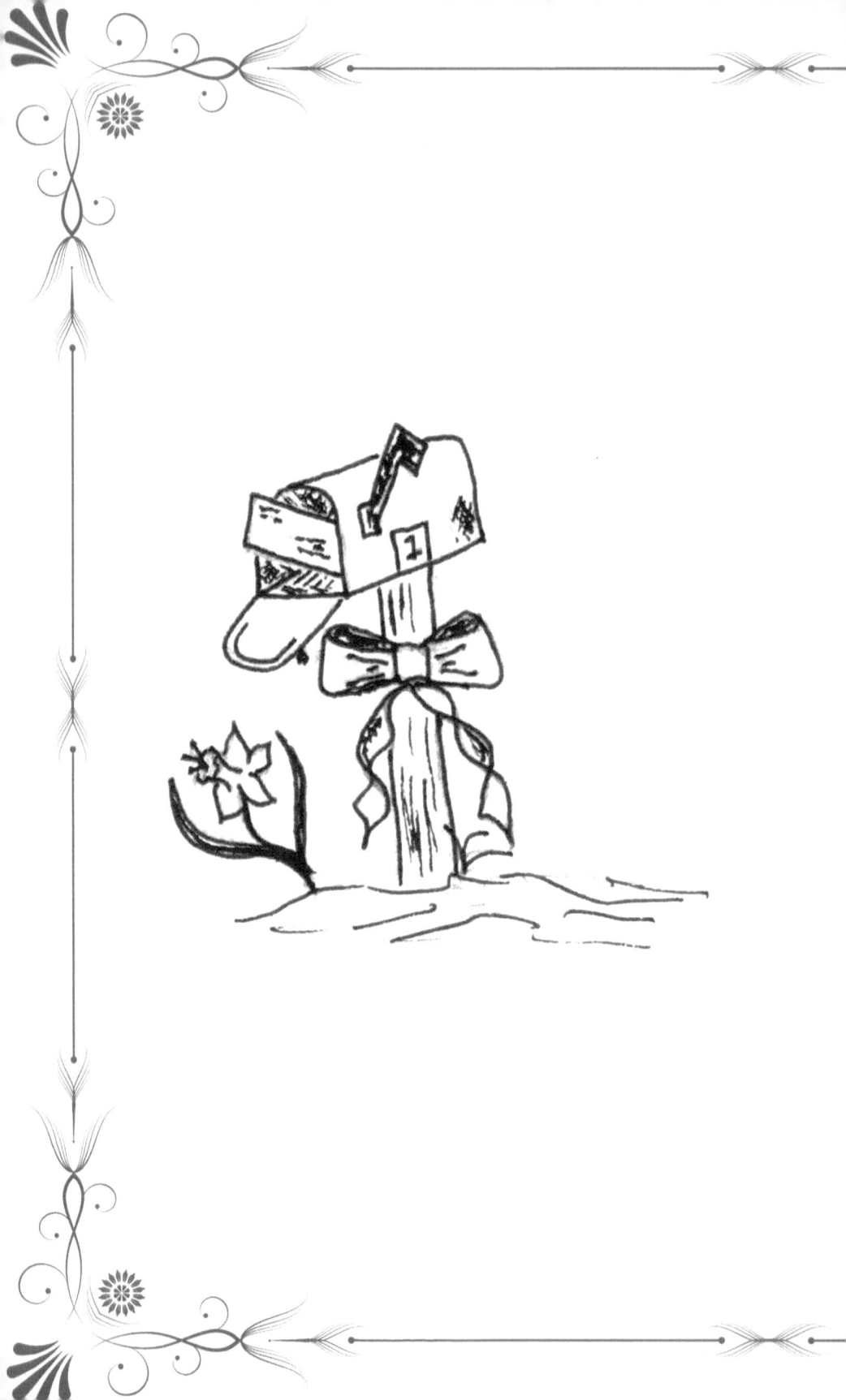

Yellow Ribbons

Yellow ribbons all around
Like warmth of summer sun,
Streaming rays to guide our troops
Back home when they are done.

Golden bows on mailboxes
Lemon strands on trees,
Can you feel it, U.S. troops?
It's your country that you please.

There are huge bows on our school signs
Other pass on trucks,
Like yellow birds they fly on by
There meaning though has struck.

Butter yellow sunbeams
Also do their part
Decorating winter skies
With hope signs for the heart.

Billboards don their bright décor
With messages of love,
We support our U.S. troops
They're led by God above.